Will There Be Free Appetizers?

Musings of a brilliant idiot

by
Don Ake

ISBN: 9780998001838

Printed in the United States of America

Contents

Introduction

Welcome to my second book, "Will There Be Free Appetizers?". Releasing your first book is like giving birth to your first child. Wait, what? Okay, so I don't actually know what it's like to give birth, and from what I've heard, neither do I want to. Any procedure where they give you as much drugs as you want can't be pleasant.

So it's like fathering your first child. It's an emotional experience, and you revere and treat the book just like your baby. The second book, like the second child, is much less exiting and impactful. But there is one huge difference; this book is much better than the first.

The writing is smoother, more refined than "Just Make Me A Sammich", but provides plenty of laughs. There are more thought-provoking essays, and some of the writing is very personal. I am still somewhat uncomfortable with sharing my personal thoughts, but many of my readers enjoy this style. So, my writing is evolving and my audience expanding.

I write for only one purpose: To make people laugh. In this stressful, bitter world we all need to laugh more. I don't write for fame, and I certainly don't write to get rich. I write to make people laugh, snicker, chuckle, guffaw – whatever. And this book will indeed amuse you, humor you, and make you forget about any worries, at least for a while. I laughed out loud when I edited this book, and I had written the words!

When you publish your first book, you are filled with hope and fear. You have too much hope, but not enough fear. That's why many people may write a first book, but few write a second. However, as I launch this second effort, my hope is realistic and there is no fear. When you are an author, you write books – it's what you do. I couldn't stop writing after the first book if I tried.

So, here are the best of my favorite posts from my Ake's Pains blog, cleaned up, refreshed and organized for maximum amusement. Please enjoy!

Please check out my Ake's Pains blog at:
http://akespains.blogspot.com

Website: http://www.donake.net

E-mail donake@outlook.com

Twitter: @theakeman

📖 📖 📖

CHAPTER 1

I Like Food. We All Like Food. Why Am I Fat?

Americans are obsessed with food. We even have separate cable channels dedicated to it. We take photos of it and post it on the Internet (food porn). We have too much food, eat too much food, and are way too fat.

Because it is an absurd part of our culture, I tend to write about food a lot. When reviewing the blog posts for this book, I couldn't believe how many were food related. But when I step on the scale, the truth wins out, numbers don't lie. Also, it is telling that both my books have food-related titles.

This chapter covers a wide range of food groups: Chicken, fish, appetizers, scones, rice cakes, and cappuccino. The one obvious truth revealed in this chapter: If you really want to fizz me off, promise me food and then don't deliver! Enjoy!

Eating Miraculous Rice Cakes

The Skinny: I had serious doubts about this essay. I had just written almost 800 words on just rice cakes. However, it turned out to be a very popular post because almost everyone can relate to overeating during the holidays.

On January 8, I ate my first rice cake since the annual holiday eating binge began in mid-December. Before my first bite, I stared at it in wonder realizing what I wanted it to accomplish. I was expecting this simple rice cake to somehow attack and remove the fat that had magically attached itself to my body over the past month.

I wanted it to remove all traces of the Christmas candy, to annihilate the Honey Baked Ham, to neutralize the impact of the holiday cheeses, to unfig the figgy pudding and to de-pie the Christmas pies. Ah, the Christmas pies! Do I want more pie? DO I WANT MORE PIE? Why do you even ask? Don't be wasting time asking silly questions and bring me some more pie. Instead of all this yakking, I could already be tasting that delicious Christmas pie right now.

So I am putting immense faith in this rice cake, which has to be the most dishonest food ever invented. Cake? Are you joking? This is a "cake" in geometric terms only. You would never serve this so-called cake for dessert. You would not put candles on it and celebrate a birthday. You would never order it in a restaurant to finish your meal. No, it is a food to be eaten in shame. In the privacy of your home, with the lights off and the curtains closed. It is a cake as much as soap is a cake.

And I'm not sure it is even made of rice. Can you really tell? My "cakes" are produced by an oats company. How do we know it does not sweep up all the rotten oats left on the floor, bleach it white, and press it into cakes? And it doesn't taste like rice; it tastes like Styrofoam™, but not good Styrofoam. No, like stale, dried, Styrofoam that has been left in the sun to rot.

And this so-called food is utterly unsatisfying and not very filling. You think you will lose weight by eating these, but you end up eating ten of them at a time and then you get hungry again 20 minutes later.

These "rice cakes" are liars, masqueraders, if you will. And yet, I buy and eat this crap because I am fat. I ate too much candy, cheese, turkey, knockwurst and pie, yes, lots of pie, and that has made me fat. My body welcomes the new fat, like a grandmother welcomes guests: "Please stay, there is always room for one more".

The fat gladly takes up residence all over my body during the holidays, just like the annoying relatives who stay at your house. At least the annoying relatives leave at some point, but the annoying fat literally hangs around.

It is extremely unfair that while my body readily expands to house the fat, my clothes do not. I now wear that Spanish line of clothing – Pantalones Splitones. I look longingly at my skinny jeans hanging in the closet. They see me staring and mock me: "Someone had too much pie at Christmas, didn't he? Perhaps you should eat some rice cakes." I move towards them and they shriek, "Don't even think about touching me." This of course describes my high school dating experience in one sentence.

As I pondered this cylindrical piece of ah, whatever, I realized that I was putting more faith in this rice cake than you would in a communion wafer. I was hoping it would miraculously transform me back into a previous time, a time when I once again could fit into my pants. I wanted this cake to make me a muffin, a stud-muffin.

Yes, this rice cake is a type of sacrament for fat people. In the Church of the Hefty, this is the penance for the sin of eating too much pie. I examined the rice cake carefully, looking for an image of some saint or prophet on it, (Is that Jenny Craig?) but there was none.

People believe in the power of the rice cake because we are prone to put too much hope in things; whether it is money, houses, clothes, cars, etc. This false hope always leads to disappointment, so I'm sure I will end up very disappointed in this rice cake. (Maybe I should eat the whole pack)

And advertisers understand we are hope-mongers. They promise their products will change our lives for the better. They play us for poor, hopeful, saps. There is even a new yogurt especially for guys, the ad says it provides great health benefits and also makes you popular with the ladies. Of course, I am much too smart to fall for that crazy nonsense. But I think I may try some because it sounds pretty good.

My Appetite For Appetizers Is Insatiable

The Skinny: I knew this would be a funny blog post when I was seriously describing this event to a group of people (some who didn't know me) and they kept laughing at me.

Recently there were two networking meetings I wanted to attend scheduled for the same evening. The venues were near each other and the meeting times overlapped, so I decided to attend both.

However, I would not have time to eat before the first meeting, so initially I was concerned about being able to network effectively at the second meeting without nourishment. Fortunately, this would not be a problem as you can see from the invitation to the first meeting (names hidden to protect the guilty):

[Group Name] – EVENING SOCIAL
NETWORKING EVENT!!!
[Hotel Name]
Evermore Road
Canton, OH 44719

Tuesday March 12
5 PM to 8 PM
BRING YOUR BUSINESS CARDS!!!
FREE Appetizers!!! Courtesy of the [Hotel Name]

The first meeting would have free appetizers. It was an important aspect of the meeting and a big incentive to attend, as you can see by the use of not one, but three, exclamation points promoting these appetizers.

This was going to be a long evening, but thanks to the free appetizers at the hotel it would be very manageable. I would be an energetic, networking machine, powered by free, delicious foods.

I strategically planned to get to the first meeting right at 5 p.m. so I could get to those free appetizers before most people arrived. Last time, I made the costly mistake of arriving after 5:30. Some low-life, low-class, moochers had raided the tables and most of the really good appetizers were nearly gone. I was left with eating much more cheese and crackers than I desired.

This time would be different; I would get there promptly and then stuff my face with enough Swedish meatballs, bacon-wraps and potato skins, to satisfy me for the entire evening.

I hurried to the meeting room and was the first person to arrive. I said my complimentary greetings to the meeting organizers and then made a beeline for the free appetizers. But there were no free appetizers, just a bare, cold, wood floor. There were no tables, there were no steaming trays of food, there were no plates to pile my food upon, and there were no napkins to wipe the creamy, ranch sauce from my mustache. There was nothing – just a vast emptiness.

I felt betrayed, I felt rejected, and I hungered deeply for free appetizers. What kind of cruel world do we live in where free appetizers are promised and then upon arriving you discover there are no free appetizers? I refer you back to the invitation:

[Group Name] – EVENING SOCIAL
NETWORKING EVENT!!!
[Hotel Name]
Evermore Road
Canton, OH 44719

Tuesday March 12
5 PM to 8 PM
BRING YOUR BUSINESS CARDS!!!
FREE Appetizers!!! Courtesy of the [Hotel Name]

"Free Appetizers!!!" Three freakin' exclamation points and not one darn meatball! Will somebody please explain how this happens? Somebody tell these people the economy is doing well! There is no justification, none, for stiffing people on the free appetizers. This is America! If you promise free appetizers, I have the right to free appetizers!

I didn't ask why there were no appetizers. I didn't want to look like one of those greedy parasites who only show up for the free food. I overheard someone say that the hotel had decided not to offer them anymore. It's probably because certain appetizer scroungers were showing up early at the meetings and eating way too much. How disgusting, I hate those types of people; I mean come on, show some class! And apparently someone was too lazy to call the hotel and confirm that appetizers would be served before issuing the "three exclamation point !!!" invitation.

Since there were no free appetizers, I left early and very hangry for my second meeting. As I sat at the traffic light, I saw the sign for "The Tilted Kilt". They have good appetizers, but they are not free. The restaurant name is deceptive, however. I thought it was a place when Scottish men could wear Scottish garb, eat haggis and hoist an ale. But it turns out that it's the waitresses who wear the kilts, but their outfits run a couple sizes too small and sometimes the kilts get tilted.

This provides some magnificent views of the geography of Scotland, including the mountainous Scottish Highlands, the Scottish Lowlands and an occasional peak of the Southern Uplands. You never do get to see the Inner Hebrides* however, because it is a classy joint.

I decide to eschew the tour of Scotland and continue down the road. But, at the next light I could see the "Ta Ta Tavern" up ahead. This place is always advertising free appetizers. I'm sure the appetizers are hot, spicy and mouth-watering and the ladies working there are ho …, okay you get the idea. Now while the appetizers are free, I'm guessing the dancers are not. I'm sure they are proficient at satisfying certain appetites, but I decide to proceed to the meeting.

Unfortunately, the people at the second meeting find my plight of being stiffed on free appetizers rather amusing. None of these cheapskates offered to buy me any appetizers (which would then be free for me). They suggest that perhaps I should blog about it, which is a stupid idea. Who would want to read an entire post about … oh never mind.

By the time I leave, I am famished. I make sure not to drive past that "tavern" on the way home. Maybe I could go home and demand that my woman make me a sammich. Instead, I decide to do carry-out at Taco Bell. Taco Bell is also very deceptive. They tell you to "make a run for the border". I would never get there because I always have to "make a run for el baño" after I eat.

Interestingly, a few weeks later I found myself in the same predicament. I had two events on the same night and needed ample food to make it through. The first event advertised a "reception" which means you get to "receive" some interaction with people. But much more important is "receipting" some free appetizers.

And this time, my free appetizer expectations were greatly exceeded. It was a high-class selection of delectable foods, most of which I could not identify, even after eating it. There were choices from the six main food groups, including bacon. It was so complete, there was even asparagus. I hate asparagus. It's disgusting. But it was a nice touch. Incredibly, I was the first person in line for these awesome, delectable, free appetizers. So I got the first bite of the apple, and everything else, except for the asparagus of course.

I love free appetizers!

My faith in free appetizers has been restored, thanks to my friends Matt and Willy, who were responsible for providing this feast. These guys understand the concept of free appetizers and know how to deliver the goods. So if anyone is holding an event which includes free appetizers, please send me an invitation.

* *The Hebrides are islands off the west coast of Scotland. Hey you learned something! This book is educational too!*

Might As Well Face It, I'm Addicted To "Cap"

The Skinny: I always make fun of people who buy expensive coffees every day. However, it is a good thing I have never worked near a coffee shop or I would need some serious coin to pay for my cappuccino addiction.

I got a work email just before midnight on Monday informing me that Tuesday's morning staff meeting had been moved to 9 a.m., 30 minutes earlier than usual. While this was short notice, I work from home, so joining the conference call at 9 a.m. normally causes no problems whatsoever.

But I had a dentist appointment Tuesday morning, and this created a serious situation. Right down the street from the dentist is a coffeehouse that brews a most exquisite cappuccino. After my appointment, I reward myself with a steamy, delightful treat. I actually look forward to going to the dentist just because of the cappuccino. However, this morning if I stopped for my cappuccino, I might not make it home on time to join the staff meeting.

You might think this is not a big deal, but you would be wrong. I love cappuccino. I love smelling cappuccino, I love tasting cappuccino, I love ordering cappuccino. I even love saying the word, I even love typing it: cappuccino, cappuccino, cap-puccinoooooooooo. Booyah!

At a former job, the company would provide free coffee out of the vending machine on Monday if the factory had no accidents for 30 days. Fortunately, the machine made a decent cappuccino. The free coffee was designed as a reward for the factory workers, but I would find a way to sneak four free cappuccinos up to the front office every Monday. It was like free appetizers only in liquid form. (For some reason, I never slept well on Monday nights.)

Of course, it was always a tragedy when there was an accident in the factory and the free coffee was taken away until there was a new 30-day period.

Everybody would be like: "Poor Hank, he got his arm ripped off by the milling machine".

I'd be like: "Dang, no free cappuccino for at least a month. What an idiot!"

I figured if the dentist appointment went quickly, I could get the cappuccino and still call in on time. If the appointment ran unusually long, I would miss the meeting altogether and there would be no problem stopping for the cappuccino. However, if the visit ran right on time, I would have an excruciating decision to make.

Naturally, the appointment was uneventful and ended right at the expected time. I stared at my watch and sighed.

Meeting or Cappuccino?
Meeting or Cappuccino?
Meeting or Cappuccino?
What to do? What to do? What to do?

There was a time in my younger days when this would have been a no-brainer. I would have put the company's needs before mine. I would have towed the company line. I would have tried to please my boss so that I could curry favors and get huge raises and promotions. I would crave getting massive kudos and accolades! Yes thir, yes thir, yes thir!

But then years later, you run into your former butt-head boss clerking at the Home Depot because that's the best job he can get now. You realize he really was a worthless piece of crap when you worked for him and how utterly ridiculous it was to pander to him. So ironically, for years this jerk put the screws to you, now he's fetching screws for you.

But still.................................
MEETING or CAPPUCCINO?
MEETING or CAPPUCCINOOOOOOOOOOOOOOOOOO?

I'm not saying I'm proud of my decision, but the photo shows the choice. Come on, was I really going to drive past the coffeehouse without getting a cappuccino? I'm incapable of doing that. I know this is wrong, so wrong. But if this is wrong, I don't want to be right. What I want is a hot, delicious cappuccino. I don't even remember turning the steering wheel. I think the car drove to the coffeehouse on its own.

Might as well face it – I'm addicted to cap

I do have justification for this highly irresponsible decision. Yes, I could have made it to the meeting on time, but I would have been in a horrible mood all day because I got no cappuccino. I may have been insensitive or yelled at important customers and caused the company to lose boatloads of business. Being a true company man, I could not take that risk. This drink was actually an investment in the company's success. Heck, I should have put it on my expense report. Hey, cappuccino this exquisite isn't cheap!

So, I got a hot, steamy, creamy, cappuccino. The good news is there was no line at the coffeehouse and I made it to the meeting only a few min-utes late. I muted my phone to drown out the moans of passion as I dipped my tongue into that frothy sweetness. I'm sure there was important business discussed in the meeting, but I have little recollection of it. I was way too enthralled enjoying my cappuccino. Hopefully someone took good notes.

There are many essential things in life and plenty of important decisions to make, but as a middle-aged guy, I have developed this wise philosophy of life:

Sometimes you just have to stop and drink the cappuccino..........

The Fat: My dentist loves this post. I now refer to him as "Dr. Cappuccino".

Dr. Cappuccino

My Superiority Is Carved In Scone

After a recent dentist appointment, I stopped at my favorite coffee shop/bakery to reward myself with a delicious cappuccino as I always do. As the barista was preparing my drink, I realized I needed something for breakfast and perused the offerings.

To my left, I spotted two humongous muffins. No, I am not referring to the waitress (and how dare you think I was), although she wasn't a flatbread. These literal muffins were indeed huge, but perhaps too big. Even if the muffins were tasty, there was just too much muffin. I know some guys will claim muffins can never be too large, but I decided to pass on the muffins.

To my right, were a cornucopia of baked goods. There were the standard cupcakes, pastries, etc. Then I noticed a platter with four wedge-shaped confections. The sign below read, "Scones $3.00".

Scones? I had heard of scones. Isn't this something that queens nibble on with their afternoon tea? I didn't know scones still existed. I wasn't even sure they were legal in the great-again United States. But the scones intrigued me. Why were they $3? They looked overpriced. The muffins were only $2, and they were much bigger than these flattish wedges. I should get the muffin, I thought.

Yet, the urge to try something new was pervasive. The barista returned with my cappuccino and asked if I wanted anything else.

There were different toppings on the scones, so I assumed there were different flavors. I did not want the barista to know I was a scone-virgin. I wanted to appear as a debonair scone connoisseur, a man of the world, who had tasted many, many, scones. Of course, even being concerned about how a bakery employee perceives me reflects a personality flaw I'm sure would keep a therapist intrigued for years. But, I'll never see a therapist, because I fear after the first session I would be locked up and heavily medicated, and who needs that?

So, I look confidently into the woman's eyes, turn, gesturing toward the scones, and with my best Raymond Reddington (The Blacklist) voice and expression:

"The scones, what types do you have?"

She promptly rattles off the four flavors. A couple were fancy. I'm in new territory here, so I keep it very simple.

"Lemon, please get me the lemon."

She wrapped up the scone and I realized I had just paid $3 for some unknown, apparently fancy food. The scone was heavier than I expected, maybe I had spent $3 for a lemon rock. I hope it doesn't bust my teeth, which would be ironic, coming home from the dentist and all that. However, as I left the store with my cappuccino in one hand and the scone in the other, I suddenly felt exceptional. This just wasn't a typical glorified yuppie experience, no, I was dignified. I, Don Ake, was eating a scone for breakfast and it would change my entire day.

There was a new hop in my step as I went to my car, not quite a strut, but much more pronounced than my usual gait. When I motioned a driver to go ahead of me in the parking lot, instead of the standard side-wave of my hand, I gave her a stately, two-finger salute and a "pip pip cheerio". And inexplicably, I began to think to myself in a British accent. By George, I started feeling rather chipper and distinguished, I did.

I was so excited about my scone, I never touched my cappuccino on the drive home. When I realized this, I worried that the two flavors might be in conflict. An English baked good with an Italian drink, ugh, I didn't want to have a reenactment of World War II in my stomach.

I'll never forget that first bite. Intense lemony bread, melting in my mouth, overwhelming my taste buds in an extremely delightful manner. This is more than just a royal delicacy. It is the breakfast food of the gods. Oh my! Yes, it was $3 really well spent. It was so tasty that I didn't even drink much of my beloved cappuccino as to not dilute that incredibly delicious lemony flavor.

After devouring the scone and finally enjoying the cappuccino, a strange sensation enveloped me. Suddenly I felt highly elevated, privileged and empowered. This was status food. It had fed my stomach and also fed my ego! I imagined myself superior to everyone else (Okay, I realize I always feel this way, but the scone made it more intense). It was almost as if I possessed magical powers. That book should have been titled: Harry Potter and the Sorcerer's Scone. I was confident I could achieve anything I attempted that day.

I began my work day (I work from home) and was soon involved in a debate with my co-worker Ron. Silly Ron thought we should decrease our forecast 50 basis points because the Philly Fed Coincident Index had weakened. I argued that the forecast should be increased 30 basis points on the strength of the Diffusion Index. Everyone knows the Diffusion Index is a far superior predictor than the stupid Coincident Index, but Ron wouldn't listen to me. We kept debating this issue and neither one of us was going to give in. Exasperated, I used a new tactic:

Me: What did you have for breakfast?
Ron: I had toast.
Me: That's what I thought. Well, I had a scone,
so we are going to raise that forecast, you see.
And we did raise the forecast because what could he say?
I mean, I had a scone for breakfast and he only had toast.

Later in the day, I called my cable company over a disputed charge on my bill. The rep refused to listen to my explanation, so:

Me: Do you realize who you are speaking with?
Rep: You said you are Don Ake.
Me: You are speaking with someone who happened
to have a scone for breakfast.

Rep: You had a scone?
Me: A large, lemon, scone.
Rep: I will remove that charge from your bill at once, Mr. Ake and throw in a free month of Showtime. I am so sorry about our error, it won't happen again.

Late in the day, my stockbroker called me with a hot tip.

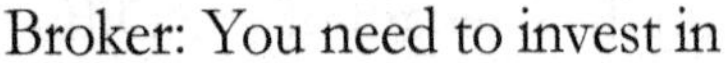
Broker: You need to invest in
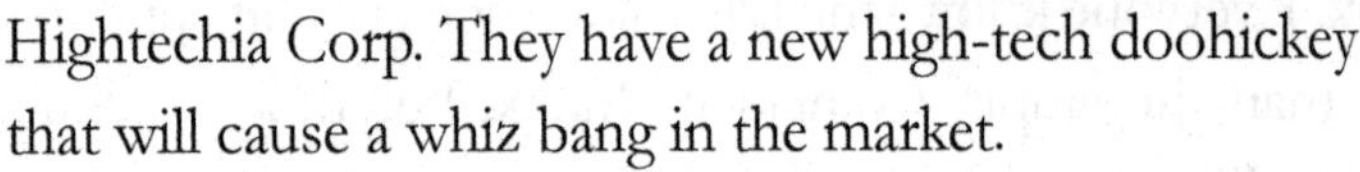
Hightechia Corp. They have a new high-tech doohickey that will cause a whiz bang in the market.
Me: I think I should invest in Amalgamated Scone and Strudel
Broker: What! Are you stupid? A bakery instead of high-tech?
Me: What did you have for breakfast?
Broker: Cereal
Me: Of course you did. Well, I had a scone for breakfast, so buy some Amalgamated Scone and Strudel right now.
Broker: What's the ticker symbol on that?
Me: It's "A" something, something.

So you see, eating a scone for breakfast changed my whole day for the better. You can be sure I will be stopping back soon to sample more flavors. In addition, I am now prepared if I ever get invited to have tea with the Queen. The scone is truly an amazing food.

There Is Something Fishy About Lent

The Skinny: I don't often write about religion because everyone is too darn sensitive. Here, I wasn't making fun of anyone's faith, but pointing out the absurdity of how we try to follow this old rule in our modern culture.

I noticed many people eating fish on Friday for Lent. A wondered why this was happening, and a friend told me he does this to be pious. Well, I want to be pious and I don't want other people to be more pious than me. No sir, I want to be exceptionally pious. I want to be the epitome of piousness. Therefore, if these people are eating fish on Friday, so am I. My friend did caution me, "Remember, this is Lent, so it all has to do with sacrifice".

I was eager for the next Friday to get here so I could begin my pilgrimage to piety. I went to my favorite seafood restaurant, but was faced with an arduous choice. Should I get the Blue Fin Tuna? Perhaps the Red Snapper Livornese? The Baked Dijon Salmon looks simply decadent, whoa, better scratch that one. I don't want to be decadent during Lent, do I?

I choose to sacrifice with the Pan Roast Sea Bass, imported of course, with the stuffed courgettes. Now you may not think this meal was burdensome, but it took considerable time and effort to truly savor the scrumptious flavor of the sea bass. And the peppers stuffed in the courgettes caused some gastric discomfort, which was a hardship for me and those close to me as well. Although I don't believe this qualifies as burnt offerings.

You may not consider this the holiest of meals. However, I must point out the courgettes were sprinkled with olive oil just like they use in the Holy Land. And finally, the imported sea bass strained my credit card limit. So this meal had many sacrificial aspects. Pious, extremely pious.

But, as I left the restaurant, I did not feel holy and sanctified. I felt stuffed, as stuffed as those courgettes, which were magnificent by the way. Maybe I was going about this wrong. I decided to try something different the following week.

That Friday I visited the local fish fry at the church down the street. This is perfect I surmised. If eating this fish makes you righteous, then what better place to consume it than in an actual church building? Plus, I would be hanging out with the pious crowd and perhaps some of their piousness would rub off on me.

It was an all-you-can-eat deal, but after eating two large pieces I was full. I was about to leave when I saw the guy at the table next to me get a third piece of fish. What? If eating fish produces piousness, then the more fish you eat, the more pious you become, right?

I was not going to let this guy be more righteous than me. I am so righteous. If I had a brother, we would be the Righteous Brothers. Actually, we would be the Ake Brothers, but you get the idea. I was not about to let this schmuck out do me, so I ate a third piece, and a fourth and a fifth, matching him filet by filet. But I could not finish the seventh piece and I watched in dismay as my adversary devoured his eighth. Oh yeah, this guy was righteous all right. I'm not worthy. He did have this aura of holiness around him, just like the Buddha. Come to think of it, he looked a little like the Buddha, I wonder?

I waddled to my car, sad that my second attempt to achieve piety had also failed. By stuffing my face full of fish, not only had I not achieved virtue, the opposite had occurred. I had committed the sin of gluttony. It was then I realized something was seriously wrong.

Yes, something is suspicious here. Something is strange, something is dubious. Something doesn't smell right. It smells wrong, it smells…, it smells …. Sorry, I just can't come up with a good word to describe it.

So I am declaring "Shenanigans" on all this fish eating nonsense! How is this a sacrifice when this stuff tastes so good. And if it doesn't taste good, dip it in some tartar sauce, the universal antidote for bad tasting fish. How can this be a penance when it tastes much better than what people eat it Third World countries? (Especially with a side of coleslaw) Shenanigans, I tell you! MAJOR SHENANIGANS!

If you truly want to sacrifice, eat tofu on Fridays. Or how about a nice big kale salad? How about some of that quinoa crap? Eat that stuff all day and you will not only sacrifice your Friday, but spend most of Saturday morning getting "cleansed", and I don't mean spiritually.

If you want to actually obtain nirvana, eat a vegetable burger. And not one of those generic veggie burgers. No, eat one that contains pieces of multi-colored gunk in it, so you have no idea what you are ingesting. It's like the ultra-modern version of mystery meat, only it's not even meat. It's gobs of who-knows-what, fused together into patty form and scandalously called a "burger". Like it resembles a cheeseburger in any aspect but its geometry.

If you can eat that monstrosity and not "ralph" it up, you have accomplished something. Perhaps you are spiritually pure.

Therefore, I have made a new Lenten resolution. I will march to the beat of a different drummer. I will take the road less traveled. I will swim against the tide. When everyone turns to the left, I will turn to the right. That is correct: I am giving up fish for Lent! Unless of course, I can persuade someone to make me a fish sammich, I just might be tempted to indulge.

The Fat: There were no negative comments about this one, so I assume people realized it is all in fun and had a good laugh!

But There Will Be No Chicken

The Skinny: It is interesting how we can anticipate the simple pleasures of life and then become disappointed when things go wrong.

I was all giddy with excitement anticipating going to a fantastic holiday party that evening, when I received disturbing, gut-wrenching, news. An email appeared mid-morning announcing the party had been cancelled due to "severe" weather.

I was perplexed by this and quickly checked the forecast which said the evening temperature was expected to be around 9 degrees. Now I was really befuddled, because in Northeast Ohio, 9 degrees is something we refer to in wintertime as, "chilly".

When I realized the full implication of this ridiculous decision, I became enraged. The party, put on by an organization I belong to, features a delicious potluck dinner, including chicken which is paid for with our dues.

But this is not ordinary chicken. It is perhaps the finest chicken ever. I had been anticipating this scrumptious chicken all week. The party was just a few hours away, and I was already craving devouring that chicken. And now: I have paid for chicken, but there will be no chicken. None, no chicken.

I assure you, I am not being unreasonable here. This chicken is exceptional. It is "broasted". I have no idea what that means, perhaps that a bro roasted it? It is covered in a tasty, crunchy, delightful coating which melts in your mouth. The chicken itself is not too juicy, not too dry, it is perfect chicken. It is carefully packaged in aluminum containers which keeps it hot until that luscious, juicy chicken hits your taste buds. This is chicken nirvana. It is an awesome chicken experience. However, I will not be experiencing this joy, because: I have paid for chicken, but there will be no chicken.

Of further concern, I had bought and wrapped a present for the "white elephant" gift exchange, but I won't be able to exchange it with anyone because the holiday party is cancelled due to someone in Northeast Ohio who mistakenly believes that 9-degree temperatures are "severe".

Unfortunately, I cannot give this gift to anyone as an actual Christmas present because it is in fact a piece of crap. A very crappy gift. Big crappy, woefully crappy. And it is a crappy gift because of the pitiful, cheapo, $6 spending limit. What the heck can you buy for $6 that isn't just a piece of crap? You end up spending valuable holiday time shopping for something crappy in order to get something equally crappy in return. What sense is that? The big "white elephant" has just taken a big white crap on all of us.

I can't even give something this crappy to my newspaper delivery guy, lest I risk next Sunday's paper being strewn all over the street imprinted with tire tracks when he repeatedly backs up over it. Likewise, if I give this crappy gift to my boss, I can kiss my Christmas bonus goodbye. And I don't want it for myself because it is so crappy. The plan was to stick someone else with this awful piece of crap, not me.

Making matters worse, I even bought something better than stale chips to take to this party. I didn't have time to go to the dollar store for the usual awful snacks, so instead I bought some festive Christmas cookies. Of course, these are just regular cookies with red and green icing and sprinkles on them. In July, you can buy the same cookies with yellow icing and they are labeled just "cookies". But put red and green icing on them, and by the magic of the season, they are miraculously transformed into festive Christmas cookies! This means they cost more, but they do seem to taste better, because it is Christmastime, after all.

However, now I am stuck with all these cookies because 9-degree weather is apparently too severe. Normally, having many leftover cookies would be a wonderful thing. But my house is currently filled with an enormous amount of homemade "real" Christmas cookies which will last me until mid-February. Regrettably, these store-bought cookies are technically only Christmas cookies due to the icing and sprinkles. While these cookies would be considered tasty when covered with yellow icing in July, they are downright awful when compared to genuine Christmas cookies. They are, what's the word.... what is it? Oh yeah, they are crappy. Very, very crappy cookies. So crappy, that I will feed these to the dog. The dog will eat them too fast and then "ralph" them up on the carpet. Not to worry, the barf will be red and green, Christmas barf if you will. Which somehow makes it better and adds to the joy of the season.

I will also miss the comradery of celebrating with my fellow group members. Last year's party was so much fun. Especially when a few of the young women drank a little too much "holiday punch" and started to get a bit "frisky". I had to step in and attract all of their attention so that the young guys in the group would not take advantage of this precarious situation. Yes, it was burdensome (so much giggling), but that's the type of guy I am. Always there to help.

But the worst part by far is: I paid for chicken, but I will get no chicken. None.

To be fair, the wind chill was negative 6 degrees. However, it only feels that cold if the wind hits your skin. When it is this cold, many people use some recently invented garments for protection, including the winter hat (invented around 1870) and the winter gloves (invented in the 1600s). These would be adequate to keep someone from freezing during the brutal 50-foot walk from the parking lot to the building.

Reportedly, breathing air this cold can be damaging to some individuals. And that's fine, they could stay home, while the rest of us dine on scrumptious chicken. It would have even been preferable, because if fewer people show up, there would just be more chicken for everyone else. Maybe there would even be some leftover chicken that I could take home with me after the party. I know the right thing to do would be to drop off the extra chicken at the homes of the unfortunate people who were not able to attend the party, but trust me, that will never happen – even at Christmastime.

Lest you think I am overreacting to this most heinous infraction, may I remind you that this is the antithesis of getting free appetizers. This is money I paid in membership dues which is supposed to be used for incredibly delicious chicken of which I will not get any. You see: I have paid for chicken, but there will be no chicken.

And there will be no refund of my membership dues since the year has ended. No chicken and no refund. Yes, I have contacted my attorneys Buckham, Duckem and Fukaro, but they are not returning any of my calls. No doubt, they are attending holiday parties which were not cancelled due to "severe" weather and feasting on higher class foods such as shrimp, lobster and pâté de foie gras.

Do you understand what I am trying to say? I PAID FOR DELICIOUS, MOUTH-WATERING, BROASTED CHICKEN, AND THERE WAS NO FREAKIN' CHICKEN! NONE, NOT EVEN A WING!

To conclude, my entire Christmas season this year has been ruined by one unfortunate incident, in which: I paid for chicken, but I got no chicken.

The Fat: I did leave this group over this most unfortunate incident. I have principles, you know.

🕮 🕮 🕮

CHAPTER 2

I Am A Son Of A Beach

I was 40 years old when I visited an ocean beach for the first time. Obviously, my parents weren't beachcombers, and neither was I. I really don't like the beach. It is hot, humid, and much too sandy. I often get sunburned and I don't go into the ocean much (eww, what's that on my foot?)

However, my wife absolutely loves the beach. It's the place she relaxes and de-stresses the best, and that is the purpose of our vacations now that our children are grown. Therefore, it is an easy compromise. If I want a happy, relaxed wife, I vacation at the beach. We have vacationed at a beach almost every year since 2001. We now visit three times a year. Happy Wife = Happy Blogger!

There are also many weird people, wearing weird outfits, doing weird things on the beach. Because the beach is part of my life and people-watching is a passion, it is not surprising that I write numerous posts about the beach. (If you're reading this in the winter, I hope it warms you up!)

Really Colin? You Stupid Son Of A Beach (My Vacation Is Ruined Part 1)

The Skinny: I don't like to write blog posts when I am on vacation. Vacation is for powering down my brain and relaxing. How-

ever, being cooped up due to bad weather, I wrote this because I had nothing better to do. I sat facing the window, so I could draw inspiration from the storm.

People enjoy my posts, because even when I obsessively whine about something, they can relate. So even if your vacation was mediocre this year, it is still better than this one.

I looked forward to my summer vacation for weeks. I desperately needed relief from the stress of being a best-selling author (okay, well, the best in my neighborhood at least) and a well-respected, industry expert (yeah, really). This year's destination was Sarasota, Florida's Siesta Key beach, recently named the second-best beach in the entire country!

But today, as I write this, it is not the second-best beach in the U.S. In fact, it is not a beach at all. It is a cesspool of heavy rain water swirling with the white sands, caused by something awful called Tropical Storm Colin.

Unfortunately, today, Siesta Key would be rated well behind the beach closest to my home. That one is located on Lake Erie, something the locals call the North Coast. The beach on Lake Erie is horrendous. It is cloudy with a cool wind, and it is covered with craggy rocks which can pierce your buttocks if you are not careful where you sit. The water is filled with a ghastly mix of industrial chemicals. You are fortunate if you do not grow a third eye after swimming in the lake. But today, I could actually be enjoying my vacation on that beach without paying for costly plane tickets or renting an excessively expensive condo.

Today, my current location would also rank behind the Jersey Shore known for its wide variety of washed-up debris, including used condoms. "Look dad, I found a jellyfish!" When your beach is ranked below used condoms, you are at a lousy beach.

And this must be a freak tropical storm, because I am not in the tropics, I am in Florida, for St. Petersburg's sake. It's part of the United States. This storm could be caused by global warming, but it should absolutely not be happening right here while I am on vacation. This is just the type of injustice Donald Trump is promising to fix.

And why would there ever be a tropical storm near the ocean? The ocean already has enough water. It has plenty. Why would it need any more? But it is getting more, lots more, torrents more. More rain than I have ever seen in my life. Children, what did you see on vacation? "I thaw a dolphin!". "I thaw a pelican!" And how about you Donnie? "I thaw a freakin' tropical storm!"

This is a historic storm, the earliest in the season for one starting with the letter "C". I guess I should feel some prestige in being a part of this momentous event. Yeah, like being a passenger on the Titanic. I should buy a t-shirt that says: "I Vacationed In Florida During Tropical Storm Colin"

They claim the storm started off as a tropical depression and I know this to be true. Because when I saw all those bizarre colors on the weather radar heading straight for my vacation resort, I got extremely depressed. If I ever meet this bass-turd Colin who is responsible for this mess, I'm kicking him square in the nuts . . . twice.

I wasn't going to let a little rain ruin my vacation, so I grabbed a lounge chair and headed for the beach as if nothing unusual was happening. In retrospect, this was a bad idea. I managed to wade to safety when the next torrent fell, clinging to the railing around the pool as everything washed away. I'm not sure what happened to the lounge chair, but I am sure I lost my deposit on it. I expect to be completely dried out sometime next week in the Northeast Ohio sun. Oh "Northeast Ohio sun"? Okay, perhaps next month then.

I'm so glad I paid extra for an ocean-side room. It was supposed to give me an "up-close view of the water" and boy did it ever, as the photo shows! I love to vacation in Florida because of all the fresh seafood, and now at high tide, it is now swimming right outside my door.

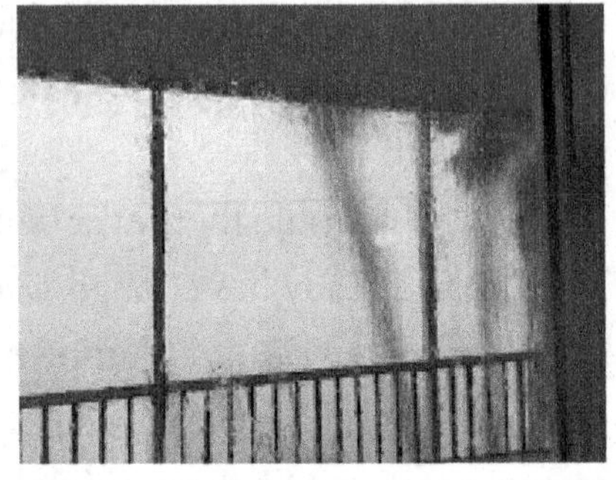

A bit too fresh, I'm afraid. And the main reason to visit this particular Florida location are the awesome, breathtaking, Sarasota sunsets. Of course, I haven't seen the sun in days. I have no idea if it ever rose or set. For all I know, it ran away like a scared little girl when the storm hit. Here's a photo of last night's sunset. Isn't it awesome?

Yes, awesomely bad.

So I am stuck inside watching multiple episodes of Judge Judy (From the case of The Sh!++ing Shih Tzu):

What a sunset!

Defendant: "You said Jerome could stay in the apartment!"

Plaintiff: "I didn't know Jerome was your dog!"
Defendant: "Oh yes you did!"
Plaintiff: "Oh no I didn't, you (bleeeeeeep!)"

This vacation is so utterly ruined. You might think I am being selfish and snobby since people have died as a result of this storm, and millions of people in Africa cannot afford a vacation as extravagant as this one. But it's my vacation that got washed out now, isn't it? I PAID LOTS OF MONEY FOR SUNNY BEACHES AND I WANT SOME SUNNY BEACHES! Besides, some of those Africans get to live on the beach their entire lives for free. So in my mind, it all evens out.

Now you may ask why I am not praying for the rain to stop since I took credit for stopping the rain through prayer at my daughter's wedding (in an earlier post in my first book). Well, I am saving up my prayer markers and picking my spots carefully. I fear I could get the Zika virus this summer since I've been afflicted twice with mosquito-borne sicknesses (once seriously). I need to save my important prayers for this possibility.

So no, I am not losing my religion, but this Colin storm is ruining my vacation. Cue the REM music:

(Ruining My Vacation)
That's me in the condo
That's rain on the window
Ruining my vacation
Trying to have fun inside
And I don't know if I can do it
Oh no, I'm bored too much

I haven't snored enough

I thought that I heard it storming
I thought that the ocean roared
I think I thought I saw the sun
But that was just a dream
That was just a dream
Ruining my vacaaaaaaaaaaaaaation ....

Bikini Madness
(My Vacation Is Ruined – Part 2)

(I am vacationing in Florida, but the vacation is being ruined by Tropical Storm Colin)

I can imagine George Harrison being on vacation during a tropical storm, gazing into the dark clouds over the ocean. Suddenly he sees a glimmer in the distance and is inspired to write: "Here comes the sun! And I say it's all right!"

But the sun is still nowhere to be seen here, and it is not all right. It is not even close to being all right. If Harrison was writing about the current weather conditions, he would no doubt be so bummed he would ingest mass quantities of drugs and write a horrible, unintelligible, song containing many swear words. This composition would not make the Billboard charts.

The worst of the storm has now passed. There is still a gusty wind and a steady rain, but this does not deter people from emerging from their refuge to reclaim the beach. However, it is difficult to describe the immense damage and utter destruction caused by Tropical Storm Colin. None, I repeat, none of the young women strolling on the beach are wearing bikinis. This is a tragedy of enormous magnitude. It is a severe bikini shortage. It is a bikini crisis.

It is June in the afternoon. It is Siesta Key, Florida, named the second-best beach in America. I am here on vacation and there are no bikinis. I am devastated by this tremendously woeful situation. The women on the beach are wearing shorts and t-shirts. But not tight t-shirts, and unfortunately the rain is not heavy enough to spur an impromptu competition. A few of these women are, get this, wearing long pants. Just let that sink in for a moment. No bikinis, long pants. And they are walking, not strutting. A beautiful woman does not strut on the beach in long pants and a t-shirt because there is no point in doing that. I'm sure some of these ladies are incredibly gorgeous, but I can't tell because there are no bikinis . . . none.

A friend pointed out to me on Facebook that I really should not complain about the weather in Florida since the flooding in Paris is so bad they had to close the Louvre. "How would you have liked to fly all the way to France and then have your vacation ruined?" they asked. This is of course kooky-talk. Because I choose to visit the sunny beaches of Florida, except there is no sun. If they ever put Mona Lisa in a thong bikini, I might consider vacationing in France (I wrote that last sentence to be at the top of the search page results when someone googles "Mona Lisa thong bikini").

But I am not out lazing on the beach. I am going stir crazy, locked inside this condo, being held prisoner by that sonnafabeach Colin. Sometimes I just stare at the walls. I even noticed the condo has a "parrot" theme. Normally, I wouldn't even notice because I wouldn't be inside. I would be outside. But now I glare at the stupid parrot wall art as it mocks me.

"Look at me pale, vacation-boy. You don't want to see me, but you have to. Caaaaawrk! No bikinis for you! But you can always check out my tail feathers, caaaaaaaaaaawrk!"

I could watch more TV, but it is a dinky 42" set with no HD. I repeat, no HD. It is standard definition. I didn't even know that still existed. And the Internet is not high speed, so I can't even surf as fast as at home even though I am at the ocean. But there is only so much "Judge Judy" I can stand. On the last episode, a woman's boyfriend agreed to pay for breast implants but only paid for one. Now she is having problems staying upright. I wonder what Judge Judy looks like in a bikini?

Author Stephen King has a $9-million mansion nearby on this beach. During a break in the weather, I sashayed down there hoping since I am a fellow author, we might share some wine and brie and discuss our craft. I was thinking I could give Stephen some pointers about how to incorporate humor into his stories to make them less scary.

I approached the gate and told the person on the intercom the author of "Just Make Me A Sammich" wanted to chat with his buddy "Steve". For some reason, the line went totally dead. It must be defective. You would think for $9 million you could get an intercom that worked.

So I stood at the gate yelling "SAMMICH! -- SAMMICH!" Soon a lackey appeared and informed me no one there had ordered any sandwiches.

"No, not sandwich", I explained. "Sammich, sammich. Just Make Me A Sammich".

He just stared at me.

"Do I look like the Jimmy John's delivery guy?" I asked with disdain.

Okay, so apparently, I do.

They keep talking about the dangers of riptides during the storm, but I think I am in danger of being ripped off. I marched down to the condo office and demanded a refund for the two days of rain during my stay. The guy refused and said there is no guarantee of sunny beaches. C'mon, it's Florida, I wasn't born yesterday. The beaches are supposed to be sunny all the time. I'm being ripped off. But when I protested again, he just glared angrily, screaming "Sunny Beaches! Sunny Beaches!" and chased me out the door.

I don't understand, that is all I want. Just give me a sunny beach please, before I have to return to Ohio! Ohio, where there are no sunny beaches and some of the bikinis sag. This has to be the worst vacation ever.

But as I write this, something miraculous is happening. The clouds have parted. It's getting brighter. Yes, it is really happening! It's Baywatch time, literally Tampa Bay watch time. Wait, is that Pamela Anderson? Whoa, gotta go!

The Fat: The last two days of the vacation were fine, and I did get two blog posts out of it!

Bad Volleyball – Extremely Bad Volleyball

I was lounging peacefully by the beach on my recent vacation when I was startled by a young woman sprinting toward me chasing a rolling volleyball. This errant shot was quite a distance from the volleyball net on the beach.

The volleyball court was a popular attraction, and the previous day I had viewed a spirited, competitive game. I took particular interest in several of the bikini-clad players who were able to successfully strike the ball despite the obvious obstructions in front of them. I greatly admired their athletic prowess and effort as their hot, sweaty bodies glistened in the afternoon sun. I imagined being out there with them, running, grunting, and spiking. They would admire my tremendous ability and yell "great shot!" when I hit a winner.

However, there had been no games today due to the extreme heat, but now apparently there was some action. I watched as the young woman, around 20 years old, retrieved the ball and returned to the court. Across the net was a man in his 40s, which I assumed was her father. She weakly hit the ball over the net; it hit the sand before dad could return it. He then picked up the ball and hammered it with full force. This time it careened far to the right, toward the ocean. The young woman dutifully ran after the ball again.

When she returned, her brother, a thin teenager, had joined the contest to team up with her against dad. And then this odd match fell into a ridiculously predictable pattern:

Dad wallops the volleyball far over the boy's head. Boy runs after ball. Boy trots back to court and tries to hit the ball over the net. Skinny, wimpy, nerdy boy is not strong enough to get ball over net. Ball goes under net. Dad picks up ball and "Pow!" There goes the ball flying down the beach again. This sequence was unbelievably repeated over and over.

This was bad, awful, disgusting volleyball. It was the worst volleyball I have ever witnessed. It may have been the worst volleyball match in the history of the sport. It was an outrage. It was a disgrace to the sport. At one point, I wanted to walk out onto the court, raise my hands in the air and scream: "For the dignity of the game of volleyball and for the sake of good volleyball players everywhere (especially if they wear bikinis), please stop!" I implore you: please, please, stop. Please stop it. You are awful at this. You will not get any better. Please stop now. Go play shuffleboard, go build a sand castle, try to fly a kite even, but do not play volleyball. You're bad, oh so freakin' bad!

But I didn't. Instead I laughed. Not the "I'm laughing with you, not at you" laugh. Not the "I am so amused" laugh. Not even the "that's cute" laugh. No, this was a mocking laugh. I mock you. I mock you so much. Your volleyball game is so utterly bad that an overweight, middle-aged guy lying on the beach is mocking you. Yes, you are that bad.

And I can certainly mock them because they were so bad that if you cloned me twice* and I played them 3-on-3, I would win 21 to 0, even in my present physical condition.

**(I apologize for even mentioning my possible cloning because I realize how frightening this concept is. The world can't deal with even one of me, so three Don Ake's would be terrifying. I think that is why my parents stopped having sex after I was born.)*

Yes, I would still beat the tar out of Team Goofups every game. I wouldn't even have to dive like those pro beach volleyball players. But if I did dive, they might have a chance to win. Because I would get sand in my crack and at my age, my crack is huge. It might take a team of trained wipers days to remove the sand and I would have to forfeit the match. But that is the only way this aimless family could defeat me.

Sand in the crack can be a serious problem for beach volleyball players. One of the young ladies suffered from this malady the previous day and had to shake vigorously to remove the debris. It was painful to watch this, and I really felt for her. I was so disappointed that her team members did not try to help her out. Rest assured, if I was her teammate, I would gladly lend a hand to remedy the situation because that's just the type of guy, and dedicated teammate, that I am.

Now you might believe that I am an insensitive cad for making fun and laughing at a father and his children sharing a special vacation moment which they will cherish all their lives. But, but, Bwaaaaaaaaaaaaaaaaaaaaaaaah! Bwaaaaaaaaaaaaaaaaaaaah! Oh excuse me; I was just thinking about that stupid guy whacking at that volleyball again.

But even in the midst of this horrible volleyball, something magical, even miraculous happened. They had a volley where the ball actually cleared the net three times. Three times! And with that, the trio declared victory and mercifully ended the match. I was genuinely happy for them and glad I could now resume my beach-induced coma, at least until the bikini-oriented matches resumed later that day.

I Wear My Speedos To The Beach

There are very dangerous encounters happening on beaches across the country this summer. And I'm not referring to shark attacks in North Carolina. No, I'm talking about middle-aged and older men parading around in very skimpy swimwear. This is figuratively a shark attack on your eyes, and once that image is burned into your brain, it is oh so tough to erase.

Why do aging guys do this? It serves the same purpose as sports cars, gold chains, too much cologne and toupees (a few losers even shave their heads). It is a feeble attempt to prove to the female species that you still have something desirable to offer: "You've still got it."

Unfortunately, you have to fish with the bait you have, not with the bait you want, or think you have. But these guys are not master baiters (well maybe they are). However, they are making a statement: "I'm still relevant as a man, so I'm putting my manhood out on fully display!"

However, these men strutting on the beach seem so confident and liberated I thought it might be fun to try it myself. So I ordered some Speedos before my vacation trip to Sanibel Island. I ripped open the package, slipped into the Speedos, and then posed in front of the mirror. I enjoyed the skin-tight fit, and must admit I looked awesome for my age.

I proudly strutted in my Speedos up and down the beach and I wrote a little poem to commemorate the occasion. (Exclusive, revealing photo at the end of the essay!)

I Wear My Speedos To The Beach

I wear my Speedos to the beach
Then I hear the women screech
I wear my Speedos to the beach

I wear my Speedos in the sun
Please rub some lotion on my bun
I wear my Speedos in the sun

I wear my Speedos by the pool
So all the ladies see my tool
I wear my Speedos to the pool

I wear my Speedos when I strut
And wiggle my impressive butt
I wear my Speedos when I strut

I wear my Speedos to the track
Move so fast they're up my crack
I wear my Speedos to the track

I wear my Speedos when I can
Cause I'm such a sexy man
I wear my Speedos when I can

I wear my Speedos in the sand
Scratch myself with either hand
I wear my Speedos in the sand

I Am A Son Of A Beach

I wear my Speedos in the heat
Showing off the Grade-A meat
I wear my Speedos in the heat

I wear my Speedos by the sea
So those chicks can ogle me
I wear my Speedos by the sea

I wear my speedos when I jam
Makes them hunger for some ham
I wear my Speedos when I jam

I wear my Speedos in the light
It fits my body oh so tight
I wear my Speedos in the light

I wear my Speedos every place
It is never a disgrace
I wear my Speedos every place

I wear my Speedos cause I'm hot
Cause maybe I still have a shot
I wear my Speedos cause I'm hot

I wear my Speedos to the park
Love to make those bitches bark
I wear my Speedos to the park

I wear my Speedos when I rock
So everyone can see my cock-a-too
I wear my Speedos when I rock

I wear my Speedos to the beach
But keep my beefcake out of reach
Yes, I wear my Speedos to the beach

I wear my Speedos everywhere
If you're offended, I don't care
I wear my Speedos everywhere

And yes, I did wear my Speedos to the beach!

MY NEW SPEEDOS BRAND WATER SHOES!

Check out those ankles, ladies!

And here is the photo I promised!

Don't stare at it too long ladies because those ankles are very sexy, no?

With apologies to Dr. Seuss. If I could f ind someone to illustrate this poem, I could have my third book. And then follow it up with: One Thong, Two Thong, Red Thong, Blue Thong.

The Fat: My mother-in-law never read this out of fear because I said it contained a picture of me in the Speedos. Despite several people telling her it was safe to look at, she refused to view it.

Reflections From A Beach I Love

The Skinny: This is the only serious essay in the book. Some people tell me this is the type of writing I should concentrate on. If you've ever had to fight your way back from a personal setback, this is for you. If you're still working to achieve your dreams, this is for you also. Enjoy.

My feet touched the warm sand early Sunday morning and I was rejuvenated. The beach beckoned me. It embraced me. It enveloped me. This is Treasure Island, Florida, and it is my beach. The sands may be whiter at Clearwater, the sunsets awesome at Sarasota, and the sunrise breathtaking at Sanibel, but I am more at peace at Treasure Island than any other place on earth. I literally love this beach. If this beach were a woman, I would .... okay, you get the idea.

But, for a while, my affection for this place had been tainted. Five years earlier I had returned from a wonderful vacation here, and was unexpectedly removed from my job of 16 years the next day. But maybe not so unexpected. My subconscious warned me of problems at work that I had been suppressing on my last beach walk during that trip.

Thirty hours later, I had much greater respect for my subconscious and for this beach. Because this beach can relax me so thoroughly, my mind can see things so much clearer. Unfortunately, I associated the job loss with that vacation because they both happened in the same week.

Now I was back on that same beach, five years later, feeling I had finally recovered and made it back to my happy place, both mentally and geographically. It had been a long, hard journey, but now it felt oh so good.

On vacation at Treasure Island, it was time once again to shut off my brain. I need to stop thinking about anything and everything. This is not an easy, nor pleasant thing for me to do. It is like powering down a large, complicated, overactive machine for maintenance (no brag, just fact). My friend Michael once asked me, "Does your brain ever stop spinning?". The answer is: Yes, once a year on vacation.

But it doesn't turn off easily or quietly. My brain resists this. It doesn't like it. It reminds me it may be needed if a difficult problem unexpectedly arises which requires solving. It also worries about how long it will take to restart when vacation ends. My subconscious on the other hand is smoking a cigar and sipping a tropical drink, knowing it will be able to speak freely for a few days.

During the last day of this vacation, on my last, long, morning walk on the beach, my subconscious revelations began flowing out. I wasn't "back" to where I was five years ago. I was so much further ahead. When you take a detour, you don't end up where you started. You get to where you need to be. You just take a different path to get there. When forced to endure, you develop survival skills and resources which are useful long after the trauma has ended.

For so long I focused on what I had lost. But it's not about what you lost; it's ultimately about what you still have. Because what you still have is much more important. What remains is what you have to rely on to move forward. It is the key to the future. At some point, the past has to really become the past. And the past, in the long run, doesn't matter, because it is … the past. Then in the last mile of the walk I had to face the issue I had had been avoiding all week. I had the crazy idea of putting my humor blogs into a book. My plan was to write one book, maybe more, after I retired. Now I had an opportunity to accomplish this life goal many years ahead of schedule.

Five years ago, I would have cowered at this challenge. I would have been afraid to fail. But I had failed so many times in the past few years. I never gave up and my perseverance finally was rewarded. I'm not afraid to fail now. After you have been knocked down repeatedly, you don't even think about getting back up. You pick yourself up instinctively.

Yet, it is a tough, grinding decision to publish a book. It is a significant commitment of time and money. It is demanding work, with little chance of success. It is having enough faith to make an enormous investment in yourself. However, I felt I had just spent the last five years preparing for this challenge, so I wanted to do this.

[The following three paragraphs were not part of the original post, but added later for this book]

My friend and fellow author Wade says you are already a success if you actually publish your book. It doesn't really matter how many copies you sell. You only fail if you don't do it.

So, on my beach, my favorite beach, in the last hundred yards of my walk, I made a commitment to publish what became "Just Make Me A Sammich". I audibly said the words "publish the book" over and over as I made a promise to myself to finish the task.

It would take another 16 months for the book to be released. It turns out that promise made on the beach was important. There were numerous times when doubts filled my head or the whole book process got so burdensome and I wanted to quit. But each time I would remember the walk on that beach, the three words, the promise. It's difficult to break promises made to others, it's devastating to break those made to yourself. And I did not fail in my mission.

My vacation is over, and I will miss my beach. Time to power up my brain and return to the daily grind. But my beach, Treasure Island, the beach I love, had once again been so good for me.

The Fat: The signature line in this essay, the one that touched people the most, is: "At some point, the past has to really become the past." This is a complex truth extracted down to the simplest of form.

🕮 🕮 🕮

CHAPTER 3

Hanging Low In A High-Tech World

The good news is that there is modern technology introduced every day which makes our lives easier. The bad news is that learning how to use all this new technology makes our lives more difficult.

And understanding high-tech gets much more challenging as we age. Heck, at one time I thought a CD player was high-tech. Wow, what an improvement over a cassette! Now I don't know how they squeezed 200 discs into my tiny MP3 player, I just need to know what buttons to push to the music come out.

If you can't remember your computer passwords, hate email spam, love getting new high-tech toys and being confused about cyber trends, this chapter is for you! Enjoy!

What's Your Password, Baby?

In 1996, my mutual fund company informed me I could access information about my account "online" through something called a "website". I had no idea why I would ever want to look at this information on my computer, but the concept was intriguing.

So, I dialed-up on AOL (if you are under 30, ask someone what this means) and proceeded to set up an "account". At some point, I was asked to create a "password"; a four-digit code, that would allow me, and only me, to access my account information. It took a while to think of four numbers I could remember and then I typed them in that special box. Immediately, almost magically, I felt very sophisticated, debonair, and mysterious. James Bond has a password, underworld spies have passwords, and now Don Ake has a password, too!

That afternoon I noticed a foxy blond at the drug store and thought to myself in an Austin Power-ish voice:

Hey baby, I have a password. I am now a crafty, international man of mystery. If you attempt to seduce me, I'm sure you can force me to reveal the numbers. Then you will know how many shares are in my Long-Term Bond Fund. Come on baby, try to get it, please, please, try.

I had one password and it was easy to remember -- and so it began. Soon I was paying bills online, each account requiring a password. Then banking and other financial accounts, still more passwords. The beginning of the new millennium brought online shopping, each vendor wanting me to set up a new account, with of course, my own personal password.

And then things escalated. More time spent online accessing news sites, organization sites and social media sites, each requiring accounts -- and passwords. I now even need a password to order a pizza. (Wouldn't want someone to order a bogus pizza using my account, would I?)

I bet I have over 200 online accounts that require a password. But this is not a problem since I use the identical password for all of them! Ha, that's a joke, but you already knew that. It is a huge risk to use the same password because a breech at the pizza parlor could result in the pizza guy draining your bank account. You have so many different passwords and keeping track of them all is freaking impossible.

The creation of online accounts containing critical information (online banking for example) began the epic battle between the Bad Bass-turds and the Good Bass-turds. The Bad Bass-turds are the computer hackers who want to steal your passwords and commit theft and fraud, and the Good Bass-turds are the IT people who try to prevent this from happening. Yes, they are "good" because they are trying to protect you, but they are still bass-turds because they are IT people, with no concept of the real world whatsoever.

Initially, all passwords were just four numbers, leading millions of idiots to create the password "1111", which the hackers nicknamed "ba-ching". The Good Bass-turds countered by requiring alpha based passwords. Of course, millions of idiots started using "password" as their password. "Yuk, yuk, my password is "password". Get it? Pretty funny, "hee, haw", to which the hackers said, "bada bing ba-ching!"

And the battle between the Bad Bass-turds and the Good Bass-turds raged on, with the Good Bass-turds making it more difficult for passwords to get hacked and the Bad Bass-turds developing more devious methods. Which led to the evolution of password "rules":

(For example, let's say you got a tattoo of a cobra in 1988)

Four-digit numeric password = 1988

Too vulnerable, so some websites went to . . .
Six-digit alpha password = cobras

Then . . .
Six-digit password requiring at least one letter
or number = cobra1

And then . . .
Six-digit password requiring the previous rules,
but one capital letter = Cobra1

Still not secure enough so . . . .
Seven-digit password requiring at least one letter
or number = cobra88

Even more . . .
Seven-digit password requiring a capital letter
and symbol = Cobra$1

And so on . . . until you get to the ultimate:

Eight-digit password requiring a capital letter, a symbol, no letters that form words and no repeated numbers = Oh, the hell with it, you lousy bass-turds, you!

(I do declare that if I ever meet the scallywag who is responsible for this particular rule, I will kick him square in the nuts, and laugh hysterically.)

Throw in the recommendations that you should not use the same password for all your sensitive accounts and that you should change your passwords frequently (although I doubt if anyone really does it) and you end up with a whole bunch of passwords, many that differ by only one letter, number or symbol.

Then comes that special moment when you are asked to provide your password for a website you haven't visited for a year. You have no idea if this site requires six, seven or eight digits, caps, no caps, etc. You have no clue which of the 20 or so passwords you now possess will work on this site. I believe the Good Bass-turds do get a chuckle out of this. In password language: URsoScr3wd!

And just to make the game more bewildering, the bass-turds add in the following challenges:

- Enter the wrong password three times and they lock you out This is very easy to do based on my examples above and can be extremely frustrating when the information you need is critical. It can cause you to scream vile things at your computer and pound your fists on the desk.
- There are websites you use routinely and have no problem remembering your password. Unfortunately, the Good Bass-turds realize this and force you, FORCE YOU! to change it for "security reasons" – but not to something only one number different – oh no, to something completely different! Bass-turds, bass-turds, bass-turds!

A solution is to log all your passwords in a spreadsheet which is dangerous if it's ever compromised. Of course, you can protect the spreadsheet by using a pass . . . oh $h!+, forget that. You can also pay $30 a year to "password management bass-turds" to handle the mess created by the other bass-turds. No, thank you.

If you work in an office, you have even more computer passwords. The IT bass-turds there are even stricter because they can lose their jobs if the system gets hacked. At one former job, I had to enter three different passwords every morning (and change them periodically) to access the computer system. I often wondered if digital security at the CIA was this tight.

If you want to fizz off the nerdlies in your IT department, and I know you do, write down your password (not your real password, but something close which helps you remember it) and post it prominently by your computer. Trust me, this will cause their heads to explode!

Here's my idea to make passwords more tolerable. Use the name of your worst boss ever and create the password "Tedsucks99!" It is a "strong" password, it is a true statement, and you will smile every time you type it!

The Most Interesting Spammed Man in the World

The Skinny: I had started to collect funny spam messages for a post, but couldn't come up with a good concept. Then my friend Brett said that whenever he thinks he is a boring person, he checks his spam folder and he feels really important. Boom! Inspiration!

You used to see that bearded, beer-chugging guy, billed as "The Most Interesting Man in the World". They retired him because he was too old. They tried to replace him with a younger actor, but he didn't last long because he was, uh, not too interesting. And I'm not interesting compared to The Most Interesting Man in the World, until you see the e-mails in my spam folder. Then I become interesting, tremendously interesting. So interesting, that I am "The Most Interesting Spammed Man in the World!"

Here is the proof:

Prancing With The Czars

A beautiful, young woman, Natalya, is a former Olympic gymnast and descendant from the Czars. She wants to immigrate and marry me so the Russian government will not seize the $3.6 million secret trust fund she will inherit when she soon turns 25. She promises to be a very willing, and flexible companion. (Did I mention she is a gymnast?!) I will have to check with my wife first, but this sounds interesting . . .

Make Love To All The Girls Near You!

This subject line could get you imprisoned for life, but it is hawking a special cologne which makes you irresistible to any and all women. If you wear this fragrance, ladies lose all control and literally attack you. It could be interesting, especially considering my neighbor Hot Carla, but I would be afraid to leave my house with the Widow Cooper right next door and Large Linda just down the street.

Mass Quantities of Boner Pills

Word must have gotten out that I was considering making love to all the women near me because the Toronto Pharmacy sent me a great offer for boner pills. They think I might be interested in their huge,120-pill package to improve my package.

Many Russian Women Want Me

Other Russian women must have found out about Natalya because dozens are now vying for my affection. One young women Inga, promises to **CENSORED** me repeatedly until I **CENSORED**. Wow, that would be interesting.

Booty Call!

Eva says she feels horny today and needs someone like me! This could get interesting! Maria is concerned I will have to spend the night alone and promises to alleviate this problem.

Five More Boner Pill Offers!

Obviously in response to all this women action on my email, five more offers for boner pills, promising fast shipping! Wow, I'm not going to have much time to do anything else!

I'm Due A Refund!

Regrettably, my recent order totaling $571,590 has been cancelled and they need my bank account number to transfer back all my refund money. I must have forgotten about placing that order, but interestingly, I'll take that cash!

Lonely Asian Girls Are Looking For Boyfriends

I have worldwide sex appeal now, since dozens of Asian women want to be my companion. It's like a digital version of The Bachelor – except I am married and these women are much younger than me. These women claim they would make wonderful girlfriends for me and assure each date will have a happy ending. That would be interesting.

7 More Boner Pill Deals!

Must have heard about all those Asian women . . .

A Very Interesting Package

UPS has informed me that I have a package for pick up that was sent from Amsterdam. I don't remember ordering anything from Amsterdam. Perhaps it was sent by one of my new international friends. I wonder what is in it! Sounds like fun! If I just pay shipping charges, the mystery grab bag is all mine. Oh baby! This is interesting!

My Recent Hotel Receipt

An exclusive, $2000/night resort hotel on an island off the east coast of Africa sent a copy of my receipt from a recent stay. There was a problem with the invoice and they needed to change it on my credit card. I'm interested to see if I ordered breakfast room service for two, since my wife was not with me on this trip. Perhaps I was with an exotic Russian or Asian babe. That cologne really does work! Exotically interesting!

A Dying Widow

A widow in Nigeria is dying of cancer and needs someone to inherit the $2.2 million her husband had deposited in a local bank. She is pleading with me to stand-in as her next of kin. I may be able to walk like an Egyptian, but it's difficult to look like a Nigerian. However, for the big money, it will be interesting to try!

A Request

Lydia wants me to treat her to my . . . OH MY! That is certainly an interesting request.

Congratulations!

Someone named Rockstar is congratulating me about something. Probably my new book! Rockstar sounds so interesting!

Indian Women Want Me As Well

These Indian women want to be my wife, but they emphasize their intelligence over their beauty, since they claim to have expert knowledge of the Kama Sutra. That must be the local community college. They sound interesting.

9 More Boner Pill Offers

(Because there are a whole lot of women in India)

Rebuilding Libya

The Prime Minister of Libya has contacted me for help in reconstructing Libya and has requested I submit a quotation of my products and services to the Ministry of Finance. So, so interesting!

An Invitation

My new gal-pal Lydia has now invited me to a wild sex orgy and has requested that I "put on those lovely navy jeans" for her. I didn't know you had to dress up for an orgy, but apparently you do for this one. I'm going to have to find some "lovely" jeans. Sounds like an interesting party.

12 More Boner Pill Emails

I need to look at these more closely in lieu of Lydia's recent invitation.

Scandalous Photos

Emails from several people claim to have photos of me in "compromising positions". I didn't know the paparazzi were following me! But unless there is one of gymnast Natalya executing a "rear dismount" with me, none of my photos would be all that interesting.

A Tragedy

Someone with my same last name has perished in a plane crash in the Andes. He has no family, and they have searched the world diligently for someone with my last name to inherit his $4.3 million estate. I'm checking this one out because I do think dear Uncle Fred would want me to get the money. So interesting.

100% Risky Free

Mrs. Koski in Australia wants to transfer $10.5 million to me to help build an orphanage. She assures me "this business is 100% risky free". She strongly believes in "no trust, no friendship, in every business" (direct quote). Sure, I'm interested in helping orphans!

Loan Offer

They are offering me $9,800, pre-approved, with 100% acceptance. Normally this would not be very interesting, except I need to: Pay to bring Natalya here, buy some cologne, secure that package, apply for a refund, date some Asians, contact the African hotel, help that dying widow, learn some Kama Sutra, buy some sexy jeans, apply for my inheritance, care for the orphans, and most importantly, purchase 5,000 boner pills!

(Cue the music) . . . I Am The Most Interesting Spammed Man in the World!

Keep reading, my friends.

I Now Have the iPhone, the iPhone 6

The Skinny: This post is from April 2015. Please consider the first iPhone was introduced in 2007 and the iPhone 6 in September 2014. Yes, I'm very late to the party, but it isn't really a party till I arrive, correct?

I have a major announcement: I now have the iPhone, the iPhone 6 that is.

I know this comes as a big shock to everyone, especially to owners of the iPhones 1,2,3, 4, or 5, since I just climbed way above you on the high-tech ladder. Because I have the iPhone, the iPhone 6.

The iPhone, the iPhone6

Likewise, you cavemen who are operating at 1, 2 or 3 Gs, the iPhone, the iPhone 6, operates at a superior 4Gs! Four Gs people, four full freakin' Gs! I was initially concerned when I first heard about the 4Gs because I thought that was the price of the phone. The phone doesn't cost nearly 4Gs, but once you add on all those fancy accessories it extracts some serious coin.

In October 2011, I wrote a post that said smartphones were a big sham and were only used by techno-snobs who just wanted to flaunt their phone superiority in everyone's faces. But I am happy to report things have now changed. What I had written before is mere poppycock, since I, Don Ake, made the brilliant decision to get the iPhone, the iPhone 6.

I made this monumental transformation by visiting a "phone store". This is where all us cool, hi-tech wizards buy our phones. I told the guy at the door I was here to buy the iPhone, the iPhone 6, and he paired me up with Solutions Specialist Jessica. I hoped Jessica was good at her craft, because believe it or not, sometimes I have problems grasping modern technologies.

Jessica was covered with several interesting tattoos. Typically, a salesperson with this much body art would alarm me, but this time I was purchasing something extremely fresh and high-tech, so the tattoos actually gave her more credibility. Also, because I prefer women without tattoos, I would be focusing on what Jessica was saying and not focusing on Jessica. Finally, she had NDB, Non-Distracting Breasts (a new term). It wasn't tit-for-tat. It was all tats and no t… (you get the idea), and in this case, that was a wonderful thing. I would not be distracted and could listen to all her important instructions.

There was an awkward moment when Jessica asked to see my current phone. I sheepishly pointed to my dinky, dumb Samsung on the counter. She grinned mockingly, the kind of look a woman gives to a new lover if she finds his gear unimpressive. (Not that this has ever, ever happened to me.) However, I will never again be embarrassed by the appearance of my phone, because I am now packing the iPhone, the iPhone 6, in a sleek, stylish, expensive case.

Jessica knew she had a challenge, but we got through it, and I was now equipped to conquer the world with my iPhone, the iPhone 6. She even copied my old photos over to the new phone, all 11 of them, giving me that same smirk again. When I expressed concern that she may have looked at my photos without my permission, I actually made her blush! Score one for the middle-aged guy. But it was just a bluff; it's not as if she would have found any naked photos of me and Jennifer Lawrence together, right? (I had explicitly denied that I was in the nude photos hacked from Ms. Lawrence's phone in my first book).

You are probably wondering why I, with my technological deficiencies, would get the complicated iPhone, the iPhone 6. Well, several times during the past year I was in predicaments that could have been easily avoided by having a smartphone. My smart-aleck friend Scott was always quick to point this out. He would say, "You know that would not have been a problem at all if you had a smartphone?" To which I would look down at the ground and mumble, "Yeah, I know". Sometimes that Scott can be a real jerk, but now he can just shut his pie-hole because I have the iPhone, the iPhone 6.

Another reason for this purchase is that I noticed an old lady in front of me using a smartphone at a recent concert! I don't care if Millennials pass me by on the technological super highway, but I do care greatly when the person zooming past me is using a walker. So, stick it granny! I'm back in the lead! Because I have the iPhone, the iPhone 6.

And I have become more popular because of my new phone. I had breakfast with my friend Tori and she couldn't take her eyes off my new phone. She even asked if she could touch it. She begged me to text her. "About what?" I asked. "Doesn't matter, I just want you to text me with that thing!" she exclaimed. The waitress at Cracker Barrel was also duly impressed with my iPhone, the iPhone 6. She got so stimulated, I thought she was going to pop a hairpin.

This phone has made me so "fly" that if I said, "But here's my number so call me" to Carly Rae Jepsen, she would call me, not maybe, but definitely. Definitely, because my number is now connected to the iPhone, the iPhone 6. And if she calls from her native Canada, that is still fine because the iPhone 6 is designed to accommodate international calls! Try doing that on your stupid Android.

There was one person who was not pleased with my new smartphone. It actually caused great fear for Kevin, the IT guy where I work (Kevin may be an IT guy, but he is not a bass-turd). Kevin has seen how I interact with modern technology. He has seen me corrupt incorruptible files, crash uncrashable servers, fool fool-proof programs, and burn down firewalls into ashes.

When Kevin found out I was in possession of an iPhone, he cancelled his own iPhone 5 and bought an Android. Even so, he turned off his phone for two days just in case. So far, I have not crashed any networks. Apple stock did go down 5% the day I activated my phone, but I'm sure that is mere coincidence.

I can now do many wonderful things on my smartphone – oh wait, hold on a minute, I have a call, a call on my iPhone, my iPhone 6. I need to take this, it might me Carly Rae. I'll be right back . . .

The Fat: Millennials did not understand this post. They didn't get why buying a smartphone was such a big deal. They thought I was really bragging about my purchase. And they were confused by the term: the iPhone, the iPhone 6. Ha!

The Many Benefits of the iPhone6 (iPhone Part 2)

My new iPhone, the iPhone 6 (this is the last time for this designation, even I am tired of it), has tons of features which I will now highlight for those of you who don't own one. Which come to think of it, is probably almost all of you. My phone has changed my life because I now have access to so many things I desperately need. It has made me so much more efficient and productive.

Before we start, I want to check the outside temperature which I can do by hitting this nifty weather button on the phone. By the way, it's 75 degrees and sunny, and as I look out the window I see that the iPhone 6 is correct!

Get this, on the iPhone 6 I don't even have to type a text message. I speak the words and they magically appear on the screen. You do have to be careful with this feature, however. For example, I meant to text my pastor the message, "I am having issues with the afterlife". You would think there would be this safety feature that prevented you from sending out a message that makes sense, but is wrong. Next time, I will be sure to actually read the message before hitting send because I did not intend to text, "I am having an affair with your wife".

Unfortunately, I was the only one who found this humorous. But it's all right, everything turned out okay. The people at my new church seem real friendly, and I'm glad to be away from the old church because of all the turmoil there since the big divorce announcement.

Hold on, my neighbor Hot Carla just posted some bikini photos from her beach vacation. Wow! I love that color on her and the pattern is really cute. I will definitely "Like" that pic.
Whoa, now I've got writer's block. Oooh, I need a selfie of that! Which I can easily take on my iPhone 6.

With the iPhone6 I can tweet about anything from anywhere. I know I don't tweet nearly enough and people really want to read my tweets. My first iPhone tweet was from a college basketball game. I was sending out an important message to my 86 Twitter followers about how the referees were making stupid calls and not being fair to my team. I had almost used up my 140 characters when I was rudely interrupted by the roar of the crowd. Apparently one of our players did a 360-degree slam dunk; people are saying it is the most incredible shot in school history. It's a good thing I had my iPhone 6 with me, so I could watch the reply on ESPN at halftime!

Wait a minute, my iPhone 6 says the stock market is down 100 points! Better buy some more GoDaddy stock. My goal is to buy enough shares that Danica Patrick agrees to go to lunch with me.

The iPhone 6 has this great alarm feature. You can set the time and the phone will ring to remind you of stuff. I use it during the day for important events and love watching the clock on the wall wind down until the alarm finally sounds. Of course, you have to remember to set it for p.m. or the thing can go off at 3 a.m. When this happened recently, my wife got upset, so I just yelled "Booty Call!" I didn't get any laughs with that comment -- didn't get anything else either.

Oh man, my daughter just sent me this funny cat video. Someone had spilled oil on a wood floor and this cat is trying to walk across it! LOL, that is one slick pussycat.

With the iPhone 6, I can make dinner reservations at exquisite restaurants right from my phone. I never eat at these types of restaurants, but if I ever do, I will be prepared.

Hold on, let me check the compass function on my iPhone 6. For your information, I am sitting facing the northeast.

The iPhone 6 has a camera that takes terrific photos and it has a zoom. With it, I took a neat picture of a squirrel that ate so much food he couldn't move. I posted it on Facebook and

got 43 "Likes". Wow 43 "Likes". My friend Graham doesn't get anywhere near that many "Likes" with his lame photos.

Whoa Nelly! Hot Carla just posted another beach pic! There is no "homina, homina, homina" button, so I'll just "Like" this one too.

With the iPhone, I can actually send real emails right from my phone. I don't even have to be at my computer. So now when I'm sneaking off to play tennis and get an important question from my boss, I can tell him "I don't know the answer" right from the court and he thinks I'm still in the office. How swell is that?!

Now I see the stock market is up 30 points, it's now 74 degrees, I am sitting a little more towards the north and my squirrel pic has two more "Likes". Wait, I just thought of something funny, I need to take a selfie of that.

The iPhone 6 has these neat things called "apps", which is short for apples, the company that makes the iPhones. You choose the apples you want, and the phone does the rest. A lot these apps are free, and you know how much I love free apps, so I downloaded around 5,000 of them. I can now tell you what city the band One Direction will perform in next. This could be valuable information to have.

For example:

Hot Chick: (Wondering out loud) "I wonder where One Direction will be playing tonight."

Me: "Let me check for you on my iPhone 6 using the One Direction app. That would be Cardiff in the United Kingdom".

Hot Chick: "Thanks iPhone stud!"

I searched for a free appetizer app. One that would send me alerts whenever there was a meeting nearby serving free appetizers. A free app app, as it were. I am so disappointed that I couldn't find one.

Rats, I'm out of time. This post took way longer to write for some reason. But the most critical thing you need to know about the iPhone, the iPhone 6 (okay I lied) is – OMG! Hot Carla is on the nude beach! I'll get back to you later……

The Fat: Please follow me on Twitter @theakeman.

I Should Have Played Pokémon Go Instead

The Skinny: The Pokémon GO game dominated the culture for a few weeks in the summer of 2016. It is estimated that over 28 million Americans were playing it at its peak. News about it was all over the Internet, and in all the other media, too.

I ran into my friend Graham at a baseball game during this time. He said he had written something in his blog about Pokémon

GO and thought it would be a good topic for mine. Initially I resisted because so much other stuff was being written about it. If only I could come up with a unique angle . . . Boom! Inspiration . . .

I wanted to join in on this Pokémon GO craze, so I took my iPhone, the iPhone 6, and searched for the app. But my eyes lit up when I noticed this brand-new game. This one was the greatest game ever created by mankind. I enthusiastically downloaded Sammichmon GO and couldn't wait to start playing.

In Sammichmon GO, a specific sammich appears on the screen. You go to various locations around the city collecting the ingredients to make the sammich. You score points for getting each ingredient, but you must locate a "sammich-making spot" where someone will actually make you that sammich. You score mega-points for completing the sammich and, of course, you get to eat it. The motto for this game is "Gotta eat them all". I love this game!

My first sammich was a basic turkey on rye. I raced around town and collected everything and located the sammich-making spot. I burst through the doors and exclaimed, "Make me a sammich!" just as the screen instructed.

The sign outside the room said "AAF". I assumed it had something to do with the American Air Force. Regretfully, it stood for American Association of Feminists, and these women were not inclined to make me my sammich. In fact, they became rather agitated at the request. Fortunately, even though they were feminists, they still hit like girls. Unfortunately, they didn't throw like girls. As I made my escape, they pelted me with all the ingredients I had collected. Sadly, I did not collect any mega-points on this stop.

Then a delicious cheese burger burst upon the screen. I gathered up everything and ran into the next sammich-making spot yelling "Cheeburga, cheeburga, cheeburga", in my best John Belushi voice, just as instructed. I did think a Hindu temple was a strange place to do this, but I needed the points and getting lots of points playing this game is extremely important, right?

The Hindus didn't react any better than the feminists, but they did hit harder, which I didn't think Hindus were supposed to do. I ran out of there with no cheeburga, no chips and no bonus points.

This game was much more difficult than I ever imagined, as I failed with the veal cutlet sammich at the PETA office, the BLT at the Muslim hall, and the ham sammich at the Jewish Center. I also failed to whip out a foot-long at the ta-ta tavern. Now two of the ladies there were eager to make me a sandwich without using any of my ingredients. They claimed they would act as the bread and I would be the … oh my! But only if I tipped them well.

Since I was failing miserably at the sammich part of the game, I decided to try to score points by acquiring hoochie-coochie, a tangy sandwich spread that when added to your sammich, earns you triple, yes, I said triple, bonus points! You get so many points for this because as the game says, "good hoochie-coochie is hard to find!" The spread comes in three flavors: Sweet, Spicy, and Hot.

The game app directed me to the local health club and indicated some hoochie-coochie was in the women's locker room. Normally, I wouldn't have gone in there, but I think Obama said it was now okay (written at the time of the bathroom controversy). So, I channeled my inner Caitlyn Jenner and confidently marched through the door. I startled a woman who looked like a Ronda Rousey wannabe. She asked me what I was doing. "I'm looking for some sweet hoochie-coochie!" I said. She threatened to do something to me that would allow me to use the women's facilities on a permanent basis. I was fairly certain that she did not hit like a girl, so I quickly ran out to the lobby.

Unfortunately, the club manager had summoned the cops. I explained to the policewoman that I was just playing Sammichmon GO. She was very understanding and released me with only a warning. Everything would have been fine except, right outside the club, my phone buzzed again. The app showed there was a large jar of hoochie-coochie in a nearby vehicle!

"Officer, can you give me some of that hot hoochie-coochie in the back seat of your squad car?" I asked enthusiastically. After a phone call to my attorneys, Duckem, Buckham and Fukaro, and paying a fine, I was back in search of some tangy hoochie-coochie.

Next, the game app sent me to the local convent and instructed me to ask, "Sisters, who here wants to give me some spicy hoochie-coochie?" The nuns explained that I was mistaken because there was no hoochie-coochie to be had there. They said they would pray for me. Well, prayers are nice, sisters, but they don't score me any points, do they? I need points, lots of points, because ah, um, well I just do.

I also struck out at the gay bar. Okay, let me rephrase that. The app was wrong again. There was no hoochie-coochie in the whole darn place!

I was about to quit playing this awful game when my phone buzzed wildly, directing me to a scantily dressed young lady standing on the corner. She said should would gladly give me some sweet hoochie-coochie, but I would have to pay for it. I told her based on my game app, I thought she should give it to me for free. An argument ensued, and unfortunately that same policewoman appeared to restore order.

Now I'm sitting in jail and my attorneys are not returning my calls. I am strongly considering deleting the Sammichmon GO app from my phone. I was trying to play this game, but I think all the time this game was playing me.

🕮 🕮 🕮

CHAPTER 4

Guys Do Stupid Stuff

This chapter contains essays related to guy stuff, written of course by a guy. You find out how a guy really feels after his sports team loses a big game. You'll hear about some of the stupid expectations and activities when middle-aged guys get together for an activity. There is a story about an unfortunate event at a business meeting that only a guy would tell. There is an essay about on what level older guys compete in the new millennium.

This isn't to say women won't enjoy this chapter. They'll like it, but they'll will be laughing at the stupid things guys do. They won't be laughing with us, they'll be laughing at us. And I don't really care -- as long as everyone is laughing! Enjoy.

The Chicago Cubs Suck

The Skinny: The morning after the Cleveland Indians lost Game 7 of the 2016 World Series many of my Facebook friends (mostly women) were congratulating the Chicago Cubs on their victory. While I knew this is what you were supposed to do, that's not how I felt. Losing is supposed to hurt and I was in pain. So I said what many Cleveland fans were thinking, but wouldn't say out loud.

Many Cleveland Indians fans are on social media today congratulating the Chicago Cubs and their fans on their dramatic Game 7 victory in the World Series. This is a great display of sportsmanship and I, too, would like to offer my acknowledgement. I would also like to express my sincere, heartfelt thoughts: The Chicago Cubs suck!

Not that I am a sore loser or anything like that, but it is clearly obvious to even a novice baseball fan that the Cubs do suck. In fact, they suck bad – really bad.

Any reasonable baseball team would have realized when it was down three-games-to-one, that it should pack it in and let the Indians win the series. Just let them win Game 5, and then go home for the winter. But not these bass-turds. Noooooooo, the Cubs just kept doing their clutch hitting, exemplary pitching, and stellar defense until they ended up winning the final three games. This is just unacceptable baseball behavior. Where is your common courtesy Chicago? I don't see any! This huge comeback is uncouth, impolite and unfair, and it is why the Cubs suck. Suck bad, suck so bad.

These vagrants kept playing the game hard. So hard, that all our good players got fatigued and could not play at their highest level in Game 7. Those disgusting Cubs even eased up during Game 7 and let the Indians tie the game. This was done so the Cubs could totally exhaust them and embarrass them by winning the title in extra innings. What a bunch of butt orifices. That's just plain mean, and further evidence of why the Cubs suck and suck big time. The Cubs just all out suck!

And the Cub pitchers are all jerks, too! Throwing all their fancy cutters and sliders right on the corners repeatedly where our guys can't hit them. Hello! It's called sports! Where's the sport in that? And our poor catcher can only hit fastballs. So, these slobs throw him six curves in a row. Are you serious? That's just cruel.

Their pitchers were also throwing way too fast, so fast that our batters were swinging at balls that were already in the catcher's mitt. There should be a speed limit on pitches. If it works on the highways, it should work on the diamond. Boy, do the Cubs ever suck. Suck big time!

And don't give me this crap about the Cubs not winning the World Series since 1908. The Indians last won the series in 1948, and I wasn't even born yet. So, there is absolutely no difference between those years to me. It could have been 1808 as far as I'm concerned, which coincidently was the first year the Indians won the series. I watched Jose Mesa blow the save in Game 7 in 1997, and at this rate I will never see the Indians win a World Series. So, I have to say, the Cubs suck. Yes, you do. You suck -- suck really, really bad.

I don't mean to be a poor sport about this, but the Cubs suck. And all the Cubs fans suck, except for my friend Jimmy C. He's okay, but the rest of you Cub fans suck because the Cubs suck. You just all suck!

And the World Series umpires, all six of them, suck. The replay officials suck. Wrigley Field sucks. Bill Murray, when he is cheering for the Cubs, sucks. Joe Buck sucks. Of course, you already knew that. And John Smoltz, the commentators, and the cameramen, all suck. Not that I am at all bitter or anything like that, I'm just saying what needs to be said.

So enjoy your trophy and parade Chicago, although I bet the parade is going to suck. You may be World Series champions, but you are very sucky ones at that. My final comment, the Cubs suck.

The Fat: I don't like the term "sucks". It has a disgusting historical connotation, and that's why you will rarely see it in my essays . . . unless I am quoting someone. Obviously, I made an exception on this essay because I was expressing the feelings of typical sports fans. The emphasis and overuse of the term here, repeated 29 times, is part of the spoof.

I do have greater respect for Cubs fans after posting this. Although this post appeared in several of the comment sections of World Series articles, not one Cub fan took this commentary seriously! There were no negative comments, so a tip of my old Ernie Banks cap is in order.

I Am The Top Wingman In The NBA

Monday evening my friend Bob left a voice mail message on my iPhone, the iPhone 6. I knew it was important because he called late in the afternoon and left a message. If it was something trivial, he would have just called back later. What could it be? What? What? I hadn't talked to Bob in a while; I hope it isn't bad news. And then it hit me! The Cleveland Cavaliers had a home playoff game on Tuesday. Bob probably had an extra ticket and wanted to invite me to the game!

And this would not be just any ticket. Bob knows LeBron James personally; there is even something about him in LeBron's book (Really!). That's right, I'm two degrees of separation from LeBron James, so I'm a very connected guy. Very connected.

I surmised Bob had been given LeBron's prime seats, right behind the bench, next to LeBron's friend Jay V. I imagined myself at the game sitting in that seat. Upon arriving I would say, "What up Jay-V, what up?", and then engage him with one of those complicated handshakes. I could then help our idiot coach by yelling out important instructions such as "Rebound" and "Get back on defense". I also would fist-bump LeBron on national television after he makes the winning shot.

Later, we would be invited to the post-game party where I'm sure there would be plenty of free appetizers. I would engage in pleasant conversation with the Cavalier cheerleaders, get some selfies with them, and then persuade them to "friend" me on Facebook (I'm friends with LeBron you know. He gave me his tickets tonight. Hey, what are you doing later?). This was going to be so great. The greatest game eva!

I could barely dial the number on my iPhone 6 because my hands were shaking at the prospect of sitting behind the bench at Tuesday's game. I hope he picks up! I hope he picks up!

Bob answered, and we spent what seemed to be an abnormally long time catching up on the events of the last few months. But, while we talked, all I could think about was:

Bob, the ticket! What about the ticket? Where will we be sitting at the game?

But the small talk continued, including a story about a death in Bob's family. I know I should have shown more empathy, but inside my head:

The invitation, THE INVITATION, I want the ticket! Give me the ticket! GIVE IT TO ME NOW!

After we discussed everything else, and I do mean e-ve-ry-thing else, the much-awaited invitation to the game was finally delivered. Only it wasn't to go to the actual game. A group of chums from high school was getting together at a bar to watch the game and I was invited to join the party.

My hopes were crushed. I tried to sound excited about this offer, but I couldn't. I wouldn't be at the game. I wouldn't be meeting Jay-V. And this bar is not one of those yuppie, hipster sports bars. It has no mega-screen TVs. There are no busty waitresses with their buns seductively peeking out at you from their tight shorts.

No, this was a dive bar – literally on the edge of town. The type of bar with sticky floors that you hope got that way from cheap detergent. The kind of place where you feel the need to wash your hands – right after you have already washed your hands. Flirt enough with the waitresses at the up-scale bars and you can get an exotic smile. Flirt too much at this place and you can end up with an exotic disease.

Regardless of these potential pitfalls, I go to the bar, anyway. These classmates are a great bunch of guys and Bob had taken the trouble to call me, so I felt obligated. However, an hour before tip-off I get a text from Bob saying he couldn't make it; some lame excuse about needing to finish a report for work. Like you can't tell your boss the report is late because of the Cavs' playoff game? No, I'm sure Bob cancelled because he ended up finding an actual ticket to the game. So, while I'm hanging out at the dive bar, Bob is probably settling in to his prime seat at the arena. Bob, you stupid sonavabeech, you.

The good news is the bar was much better than expected. It was clean, there were many TVs, and the waitress was reasonably cute. She actually began flirting with me, which of course at my age means she's getting triple the tip. The screens weren't huge and there was no imported beer, but it was totally acceptable.

But by far the best part of the evening was when my friend Chris ordered appetizers for our table. He ordered tacos, pretzel bites, cheese sticks, and lots of wings. And of course, these qualify as "free" appetizers since I didn't pay for them. Sure, I'm expected to contribute some cash when the check arrives, but while I have my debit card on me to pay for my drinks, I conveniently left my currency in the car.

The game starts, and the high school reminiscing and appetizer consumption begins. For some unknown reason, the three large plates of wings eventually ended up right in front of me. Of course, I ate a few, but at halftime I realized something very important: When I was eating a wing, the Cavs played great, but when I wasn't -- like when I was eating cheese sticks – they were horrible.

I knew what I had to do in the second half to propel the Cavs to victory. I needed to raise my game. I had to fight through the burning sensation of the fiery sauce. I had to focus on the prize. I had to eat hot wings like I had never eaten hot wings before in my life.

The game was close, so I shoved a steady stream of wings into my pie hole, taking shorts breaks to drink in order to quell my flaming taste buds. But every time I stopped eating a wing, the opponent would make a run, even taking the lead a couple times.

You may think I'm crazy, but it was no coincidence that I just finished a Hot-Spicy-Cajun trio (or trey as I like to say) when Le Bron hit the game winning 3-pointer. I made that cool three-point hand symbol, just like LeBron, only my hand was smothered in sauce.

There was celebration of this thrilling victory at our table. However, it was embarrassing to look down at the plate in front of me which contained a mountain of chicken bones. Everyone was so happy with the victory, I hoped no one would notice.

I told Chris we had brought the Cavs good luck, so we needed to do this again in the next playoff round. I suggested we sit at the same table and order the same food. Chris agreed, but suggested next time I remember to bring a little cash. I said my goodbyes and even exchanged some devious stares with the waitress.

Then my friend Chuck, who rarely says much, pointed to the last wing on the table and said, "Don, you ate the rest of the wings, you may as well have that one." While it was embarrassing to get "called out", he was technically offering it to me. So "heck yes, I want the last wing". I grabbed it up and quickly left.

The only thing left to say is if my fellow Akron homie LeBron reads this essay, as I'm sure he will: If you have an extra ticket to a future playoff game, please let me know and send it directly to me . . because everyone knows Bob is an unreliable sonavabeech.

This Business Dinner Was A Gas

The evening was going so wonderfully. A lively group of around 40 people had gathered in a private room at one of Dallas' finest restaurants. As we waited for dinner to be served (munching of course on exquisite free appetizers), the gorgeous young woman on my right seemed very impressed with my wealth of industry knowledge. She pumped me aggressively – for information, sucking hard – on my brain.

And then suddenly, quietly, without warning, everything changed. A thick, pungent, odor engulfed our area. The energetic, pleasant atmosphere was totally destroyed by someone's problematic flatulence.

That's correct. This essay is about a fart, but not just any fart, an extraordinarily unique fart as I will now elaborate.

This fart was exceptional due to its extreme intensity. My middle-aged nose may have lost some olfactory capability, but I was experiencing the most powerful emission of human gasitude of my life. It was a nasty, nasty fart.

If you unleashed this fart on the battlefield, you would be violating the Geneva Convention. It definitely would be considered a weapon of mass destruction. The room was dark, but I'm sure this cloud of thick gastric fog would have been actually visible under better lighting. The stench was so potent; I'm surprised the wallpaper didn't fall right off the wall.

This was far worse than any gas even my dog generates. It was nauseating and toxic at the same time. If I had access to a gas mask, I would have worn it. It is difficult to even describe just how ghastly this gas really was. At one point, I felt I was going to literally pass out. I'm surprised no one got sick.

The other remarkable thing about this disgusting gas attack is where it occurred. This was, for lack of a better term, a "business fart". It was emitted at a large dinner table, where I was surrounded by current and potential customers.

Under no circumstances can you ever publicly acknowledge a business fart, even though everyone is obviously aware of it. You cannot ask, "who cut the cheese?", because of the potential business consequences of embarrassing the "cheezer". You don't have any idea how powerful that person is. Okay, so you do have some sense of his power, but what I mean is you don't know where this person is on the organizational chart. For example, he might be the CFO (Crude Farting Offender). Exposing the nasty farter could cost you your job and prove to be extremely embarrassing for you in the future.

Job Interviewer: "Why were you let go from your previous job, Bill?"
Bill: "Our CEO cut a horrendous fart and I called him on it. Lit a match in the conference room and everything".

So even as this fart severely choked us all, not a word was uttered. We all had to carry on with what we were doing, pretending everything was fine, while at the same time being poisoned. You could not even cover your nose with your hand. You just had to sit there hoping you were not going to die.

Unfortunately, I was talking (I know that's difficult to believe) at the time of the atrocious fart. I was espousing my profound business knowledge to those around me, including the lovely lass mentioned previously. However, when the noxious odor hit my nostrils, my brain literally shut off. I'm in mid-sentence and suddenly I can't think straight because this horrendous odor is so pervasive. I mumble out some meaningless words to finish my sentence and try to maintain my composure. All while trying not to acknowledge a potentially deadly business fart had been released.

I assume the human body has a defense mechanism that shuts off the brain when you are exposed to poisonous gas, because you are not supposed to think, you are not supposed to speak. You are just supposed to run like hell to save your life.

Only I couldn't run. If I jumped up and ran for the door, it would be an admission that a business fart had been discharged. Worse yet, people might think I was running for the bathroom, therefore making me a prime gas-bag, farting suspect. Therefore, I had to sit in the middle of this warm, thick, fart-fog trying to maintain consciousness at all cost.

I considered saying I had to make a call and then excuse myself to the hallway. I also considered calling 911. However, I doubted the dispatcher would take seriously a report of someone at La Grenouille "cutting silent, but deadly, horrendous farts".

I feared becoming an Internet sensation as the guy who called 911 because people around him were passing gas. If I had called 911, I would have told them to bring the bomb sniffing dog, so it could point out the butt of the perpetrator. What an interesting scene and fine end to the evening that would have been. "Line up and bend over and Tootsie here will identify the guilty tooter".

But I never could identify the dirty dealer. The hot woman seated next to me was not a suspect because she was too petite to create such a dirty cloud. No, this was indeed a manly fart, one definitely farted by a man.

I do feel somewhat guilty about not reporting this to any health officials. If the guy can generate gas this toxic, I fear that he has a serious health problem and may now already be dead. If that is the case, may he rest in peace and may his family be successful in fumigating the house.

Unfortunately, they never prepared me for an evening like this in business college, not even in the MBA program. Although I doubt "Managing Business Farts" would be a popular course at the Harvard Business School. Perhaps I should write a white paper, er, make that a brown paper, on the subject.

Fortunately, I survived the nasty, nasty fart, had a superb dinner, and was able to maintain excellent customer relationships despite the challenges. The next time someone tells me "business stinks", I will tell them just how much it really does.

The Fat: Often I exaggerate certain details for humor effect, however in this story I assure you I did not. The fart was really that bad. The proof? A recent domestic flight had to make an emergency landing when passengers suffered nausea and headaches after someone passed some bad gas.

I Am Now Well Hung

"I've got a big one. How big is yours?" asked my friend Mark. I hesitated to answer this personal question, and I'm glad we weren't in the locker room when he asked. I still considered it an odd question because he could already see it. C'mon, he was even pointing at it. "It's 46 inches", I replied and waited for his response. "Mine's only 42", he conceded, giving me the victory in another round of the "Big Screen TV Male Challenge"

Today, men don't brag about their historically traditional manly skills (hunting, fishing, mechanics), education, jobs, investments, sexual conquests, or even the size of their, uh, tools, as much as they brag about the size of their TVs. If you want to be a studly man of the twenty-tens, you need to be well hung, meaning there better be a huge TV hanging on your wall.

In the olden days, men were judged on their hunting skills; how well you could provide for your wife and children. This ability made you very attractive to the womenfolk. And if you could put your meat on the table, you would be afforded the opportunity to put your meat in . . . well, you get the idea. But now in our entertainment-crazed culture, your manhood depends on securing the biggest, baddest, high-def TV out there.

In the past, Mark and I would have discussed the large deer he had killed. He would have described how he tracked the prey. Talked about the gun he used. Even become animated when he relived the shot and filled in all the details about hauling the carcass back and harvesting the meat.

But now, Mark explained in great detail how he waded

through the thick marsh of sales flyers, searching for just the right TV. He carefully identified his target, and waited, and waited. Then in the clearing, it was visible! Wal-Mart put the set on sale at an unbelievably low price. Mark blazed a trail through the traffic by the mall, securing an ideal parking spot. He climbed through the forest inside the store, navigating around all the wildlife blocking the aisles. And then he cornered the prey at the front of the electronics department. Mark pounced and secured one of the few remaining TVs. He told me this story with highly-animated, wide-eyed enthusiasm.

Yes, things sure have changed! A guy would have been proud to provide plenty of meat for his family. He then would mount the deer head on his wall as a symbol of his manhood. Now he lugs the mega-sized TV home from the store and mounts it on his . . . Oh, so maybe some guy things never change.

When I purchased my 46" big screen, I was proud and fulfilled. Naturally, you look for opportunities to inject it into your guy conversations: "Did you see the game last night?" "Ya did? Well, it was clear to me that was a catch, because I had magnificent view on my 46-inch screen."

However, as the price of 46-inch TVs dropped, it seemed every schmuck was getting one. I even saw them delivering one to my neighbor Howard, and he's a classless moron! I knew I had to take action, so I devised a plan to move the 46" TV upstairs to replace the, ack!, 27" television in the living room. Getting a bigger TV than Howard was of upmost importance, so money was no object.

I would have to use my superior male brain skills to convince my wife to spend a ginormous amount of money on this purchase.

It used to be I would spend my male brain energy for getting more, ah, intimate things. Now in the middle-ages, you just go for whatever you can get.

I waited for just the right moment. My wife was in a good mood. Perhaps I had recently done something accidentally correct or inadvertently sweet, but sensing the time was right. I pounced. I explained prices of the bigger sets had fallen. I pleaded that sports would appear so much sharper on a larger TV. Then I threw in an array of bogus reasons just for good measure. I waited for the push back, but she just smiled and said, "That sounds like a great idea". Score one for the male brain!

She then pointed out we would need to add high-definition capacity and a DVR for the 46" set when it moved upstairs. Co-incidently, this would be the set she would use more often. The extra expense for the TV is totally justified, but all this added monthly expense? Well, who needs that! My wife had totally out-played me this time. She had set a trap and I had walked right into it. Score two for the female brain.

I was really torn over this added cost thing. I didn't want to pay more charges and fees to the cable company. They keep raising the costs all the time and give you very lame reasons why. It would be more palatable if they claimed, "Fee Fairies" snuck into the computer and increased your rates.

But then I saw where a key sporting event was coming up in a few weeks, the Victoria Secret Fashion Show. It is a sporting event because these ladies are sporting some impressive outfits. And this is truly an athletic endeavor. These young women push their bodies to the limit. They make awe-inspiring moves, and the woman who can raise her game and lift herself up under pressure will be the victor in this always tight, extremely tight, contest. Wow, this would be awesome to watch in high-def on a huge TV. I was going to buy a 55-inch. But it is now your responsibility as a guy to have the biggest TV you can fit into the room. Therefore, I manned up and got the 65-incher, even though there is barely space for it in our family room. I know it looks like a frivolous, testosterone-fueled purchase, but I feel very manly now, and those Victoria Secret ladies deserve to be viewed in the best possible way.

65 inches of awesomeness!

CHAPTER 5

Cause Getting Old Is Hard To Do

I used to wonder why older people were so cranky. I mean, they would lose it over trivial things. Now that I am older, and getting older every day, I understand the frustration.

I am a baby boomer and my generation is known for its aversion to growing old. We want to stay forever young, vital and relevant. So qualifying for senior discounts, group memberships or deals on cemetery plots, can be traumatic events.

Growing old can be difficult, but it can be funny too. Baby boomers will relate to these stories, seniors will remember them, and youngins, you may not laugh much, but your day is coming. Enjoy!

I Am Not Old – And I Don't Need A Discount

It was one of those, horrendous milestone events. The type which shakes you to your core and you remember forever because it is so traumatic.

And it all started so pleasantly. I met my good friend Michael for breakfast at, what used to be, my favorite restaurant. We were perusing the menu when Michael said:

"Hey Don, look, you qualify for their senior specials!"
I peered over, lowered my menu, and gave Michael my best "what chu talkin' bout Willis" glare.
"See right here on back," he said as he flipped over my menu.

And there they were, six entrees discounted for "senior" customers, but not for ages 65 and older like most places. No, these discounts applied to people age 55 and older.

That's right, some stupid sonavabeech in corporate marketing thought they could sell more freakin' waffles if they lowered the age of their senior discounts below their competition! What a stupid, stupid, sheephead. He's probably one of those "millennials" who drives a Prius. I bet he doesn't even wear a tie to work. What a horrible idea by this stupid, despicable restaurant. How dare they charge me less money just because they think I'm old! I wanted to bolt out of the place immediately.

I didn't even look at these "special" dishes. Not that I was afraid I would actually want one. Absolutely not. I assumed that all of them came with a big glass of prune juice, and I'm certainly not interested in that.

I am not going to order some "senior-discounted" meal because I am not "old" by any means or by any standard. I am still a vibrant, virile man full of life and making a meaningful, relevant, impact on my world. By no means do I need any help whatsoever paying for my freakin' breakfast! I've got mutual funds, don't ya know?

I can't image why this contemptible restaurant believes I

need one of these geriatric specials. Do they feature stuff such as creamed oatmeal to make it easier for geezers to chew and digest? Well, that could give the old people less gas, and I certainly don't have that problem . . . okay forget I even mentioned that. Maybe the foods are high in fiber, because I've heard that elderly people have problems pooping. I certainly don't need that because I take fiber pills. Oh yeah, I know many old people use fiber supplements, but I don't take them because I'm old. I only use them for other health issues which have built up over many years . . . okay, forget I mentioned that as well.

"Are you going to get one those specials?" Michael asked enthusiastically, not realizing he was really fizzing me off.

"No, I'm not," I replied. "Are you?" (said with a bit of irritation).

"Well, unfortunately, I don't qualify for the discount," he said with a touch of smugness and a smirk.

Now I'm really fizzed off. I want to scream, "Michael, shut your pancake hole about these darn specials. You stupid, stupid, sonavabeech." But he's my friend, so I let it go.

Fortunately, our perky, chicky-babe waitress bounces over to take our order. But after Michael orders, she turns to me and says excitedly:

"Sir, did you see our senior specials?!!!!!!!!!"

Thought, but not said: Yes, you overly cheerful tart, thanks to that sonavabeech Michael I know all about your ridiculous specials. And "Sir", really? Once the young, hot chicks start calling you "sir", you have crossed a line that hurts you deeply. I wanted to tell her that even though I am middle-aged, I could still be a stud muffin, like Sean Connery, for example. Well maybe a younger Sean Connery, who was able to play James Bond and frolic with the "Bond Girls" into his 50s. I instinctively scoot towards the table to hide my un-Connery-like gut.

I wanted to tell her I could still ring her bell. Of course, I would need an hour's notice for my blue pill to kick in. Obviously, I don't really need this drug. Only old guys really need it. I only use it for a little help. Wait, I don't mean anything is actually that little. I'm just making sure, as the commercial says, it's very helpful for guys as they age . . . okay, let's forget I ever brought this up, err, I mean, mentioned it.

My fantasy was rudely interrupted by the waitress joyfully asking:

"Did you see our new Prune-tastic Platter? It's like a shrimp platter you get at a seafood place, only with prunes! There are stewed prunes, dried prunes, pureed prunes, prune casserole and a prune muffin. You also get a large glass of prune juice to wash it all down!" (Prune juice! – I freakin' knew it!)

I looked at her incredulously, at a loss for words.

She continued, "Don't worry about eating that many prunes. Since we added this to the menu, we've stocked the restrooms with 3-ply, super-soft toilet paper." Then lowering her voice to a whisper and leaning towards me she added, "Because some people who order this have hemorrhoid issues." Naturally, I do suffer from hemorrhoids, but not because I'm old. It's just from sitting on my butt in cushy office jobs for many, many ye.... okay, forget I mentioned this as well.

This breakfast had gone totally wrong. The waitress is supposed to be flirting with me in hopes of getting a large tip. I am supposed to flirt back because that's how this game is played. But now, all the waitress cares about is making me poop and assuring that it is an enjoyable experience. I now feel like I am 90 years old. I said defiantly, "I will have the Atomic Bacon Blast with a side order of bacon and I will wash it all down with a couple of raw eggs. And I want those eggs shaken, not stirred."

I wanted to prove to the chicky-babe I have the arteries (among other things) of a much younger man. Which of course I don't. My doctor is treating me for high cholesterol, not because I'm old, but because that gunk just builds up in your arteries over a long, extended time . . . ugh . . . forget I said anything about this too.

Finally, I was able to enjoy my breakfast as I stuffed my face with over a pound of delicious bacon. I leave the waitress a huge tip to prove I didn't need their insulting discount. I proudly walk past the restroom and its soft, 3-ply paper, on the way out. However, as I reach the parking lot, I experience some strong chest pains, but I think it may have just been gas. Maybe I should have ordered the creamed oatmeal after all.

The Fat: I am still refusing all "senior discounts. However, next year I become eligible for a desirable discount on tickets for the local AA baseball team. This one may be too tempting to pass up!

You Will Not Force Me To Retire

I am being aggressively recruited by a vile, evil cult. They are relentless in their efforts to brainwash me. They send messages to my television. They tempt me with radio advertisements. They run full-page ads in my newspaper (C'mon, who does that anymore?). They desire me so much, they even sent a personal letter so presumptuous it contained a membership card with my name and cult number already on it.

They target old people, probably because declining mental abilities make geezers more susceptible to their lies and tricks and much more likely to blindly join their abominable cult. But me? I am not old, I'm really not. So, I do not understand why this organization is pursuing me so vigorously.

What is this dangerous, repulsive group? They go by the stealth code name, "AARP". However, through extensive research including use of the "dark web", I discover their real name is the American Association of Retired People.

These mongrels want me. But, I don't want to join this wicked gang. I am not retired, nor am I ready to. Why do they want me so badly, and why do they want me to retire so soon? These disgusting sheepheads want me to quit my job, cross over to the dark side, and join them in some weird "association of retired people".

These so-called "retired people" walk around aimlessly like zombies all day with huge smiles on their faces because they don't have stressful jobs, they don't have butthole bosses, and they can do whatever the heck they want. This includes, get this, doing nothing at all. Sometimes I see these poor souls walking around casually at the mall like they don't have a care in the world, and it is so, so pathetic.

To this I say, "No! Heck no! AARP just leave me the funk alone!"

Yes, I know they claim you don't have to be retired to join the group, but this is just part of their evil, deceitful plan. Once you join up, you will be surrounded by so-called "happy retirees" who will introduce you to new, fun activities such as bingo and shuffleboard. In addition, their letters promise me AARP (read SENIOR) discounts on groceries, dining, travel and shopping! (and you know what I think about senior, "old people" discounts from my previous essay). They also promise big discounts on healthcare insurance and prescription drugs. Do they think I am some type of whore?

Once you get hooked on bingo and cheap Valium, you will naturally want to quit your job and join up with them. And who needs a salary when you are now getting so many freakin' discounts! These swine-dogs are intent on me quitting my job and becoming totally dependent on them. I told you it was a cult, didn't I? I'm wondering if this is just a communist plot to get everyone to quit their capitalist jobs.

There is no way I am old enough to join AARP! There is no way I am old enough to retire. No way, absolutely no way I tell you!

Okay, I must admit there are people from my high school class who have recently, gulp, retired. But that is irrelevant to this discussion. These former classmates claim they could stop working due to generous pensions or accumulating wealth by saving and investing.

This of course is hogwash. The truth is they quit their jobs because they are lazy, slothful bums. Just lazy, lazy people who lack a good work ethic. They are quitters! They quit. They had a job, and they quit. I also suspect they may already be communists. I assure you I am not overreacting to this. I've heard alarming reports of so-called "retired people" sitting for hours, in one place, holding onto a pole, waiting for some unsuspecting fish to literally take the bait. Others sit in the park and actually feed the pigeons. Please be aware these are not pets, they are just random birds. After the pigeons are full and bloated, they fly away and crap on the cars of people who are hard at work, like these slackers should be. Tell me that's fair. In addition, sometimes these retired people reportedly buy and consume ice cream cones in the middle of the afternoon for no apparent reason! How sick is that?

Because of all this lollygagging, these retired people are not attending long, super-productive business meetings. They are not developing complicated, multi-linked, macro-powered spreadsheets that are critical for our economic survival. And these malcontents are not checking their messages every 15 minutes. Heck, they may not even respond to emails for days. For days! I ask you, do we really want this?

The latest AARP ploy is to try to tempt me with a free Weekend Duffle Bag. These guys never quit with their intrusiveness. What I do on my weekend is also my own darn business, and if I need a duffle bag, I will use my own bag which I paid for with the salary from my job! Do you understand? I go to work every day. I get paid. I'll buy the duffle bag. That's the way it should work.

The AARP is most definitely an evil cult that wants everyone to retire and join them. And this is so hypocritical, since many, many people actually are employed at the AARP – yeah, think about that!

Their latest propaganda letter says they want to welcome me and my family to AARP. I say "Heck no", and you can shove your membership card and your weekend duffle bag right up your rear orifice. I will retire when I'm ready to retire, you stupid sheepheads.

This Retirement Community Needs More Life

When you start checking the dreaded age "55-64" box on all your forms, you know your life is changing – and not for the better. "You're not getting older, you're getting better" is a bald-faced lie uttered by someone with heavy, cellulite thighs or a pot belly. That box you just checked may as well be labeled "irrelevant". At this age, you are no longer hot and attractive to advertisers, but you are not yet a "senior citizen", gullible enough to be taken advantage of by all types of charlatans. Still, you do get frequent mailings for "age-appropriate" products.

But some of these offers are so totally stupid. I recently received one for a place called "Sunset Valley", which sounded like a nice retirement community. Not that I'm old enough to retire, because of course I'm not. But I do like to watch sunsets. So even though the sunsets may be difficult to see from down in the valley (doesn't quite make sense, does it?), I did check out the brochure. Just for informational purposes of course.

They claim it is a beautiful, park-like setting which provides quiet, peaceful surroundings for when family and friends come to visit. That's nice, but what about me, what about my needs? Butterflies and trees are fine, but I don't plan on being still and quiet all the time. What if I want to crank up some Aerosmith? Am I supposed to bury all my desires?

It is strange that the brochure does not mention any fun activities designed for me. Where are the walking paths, shuffleboard and pickle ball courts? Yes, I'm getting older, but I just don't want to lie around all day, do I?

They promote it as a great "resting place". Sure, I'm looking forward to taking some long naps, but then I want to rise up and do stuff. And they show no photos of the residents having fun at cookouts and parties. I mean the place just isn't very lively. In fact, it looks somewhat dead.

The brochure says plots in good locations are still available. Well I would like one overlooking the lake, but not too close to the lilacs due to my allergies. I wouldn't want to startle anyone if I suddenly started sneezing unexpectedly. I am also perplexed that the size of their plots are not listed in square feet, but cubic inches. I haven't done the math, but these plots seem to be a bit small. I don't think I want to be confined in that small of a space. That could make me a little stiff.

There are just too many things wrong with Sunset Valley for me to consider "spending the rest of my days" there. I may be thinking outside the box here, but they need to add more activities for the residents to breathe some new life into the place.

Dental Problems – Crown Me

And for some unknown reason, I am suddenly having more problems with my teeth. Of course, this has nothing to do with me getting older. It is totally random without any age-related explanation whatsoever. I think my teeth need to step it up and get tougher.

Recently one of these wimpy teeth needed a crown. I have told my wife for years that I deserved a crown, but I didn't mean one this small. During the procedure, my dentist was struggling to reach my molar, and made the most ridiculous statement ever. He said, "I wish your mouth was bigger".

Of course, he had to stop when I started to laugh uncontrollably.

"Did I say something funny?" he asked

"You have to be the only person on the planet that wants me to have a bigger mouth," I explained. "Even the people who like me a lot, don't wish for that!"

So there is at least one person in the world that doesn't think I'm a big mouth. Okay, so only one person. I'll take it.

During the preparation for the crown, the hot, young dental assistant gave me a Lidocaine shot to numb that side of my mouth. I wanted to impress her with my hipness, so out of the other side of my mouth I mumbled, "I can't feel my face when I'm with you, but I love it, but I love it."*

Now, I can't say she bitch-slapped me because she is a lady. So, I guess she lady-slapped me. She's smart too. She didn't slap me on the numb side. She got me on the side where I could still feel pain – lots of pain.

Guess I shouldn't have winked at her after the face comment . . .

No Hearing Problems Though

I get mailings for hearing aids, which is stupid since I am not old and I have outstanding hearing. There are several old people in my neighborhood, which of course does not include me, so there is a hearing aid sales guy who often comes around in his mobile testing van.

The neighbors tell me he is very aggressive in his approach. He rings the doorbell and bangs on the door until somebody answers. Well this guy must realize that I am a still a virile, vibrant strapping man with excellent hearing because even though I've seen his van parked by my house numerous times, he has never once come to my door!

So I repeat, I am not getting old. No way, no how.

**Lyric by The Weeknd*

I Am Raising Cane Over This False Accusation!

"Soon I'll be 60 years old
My daddy got 61"

"7 Years" is the worst song ever written and Lukas Graham should shut his singing pie-hole (an explanation follows at the end of this post)

BUT FIRST – ALARMING! VERY ALARMING NEWS!

By now you have seen the media reports about my scandalous involvement regarding a recent purchase I allegedly made. TMZ, Gawker, Entertainment Tonight, Perez Hilton and my nosy neighbor across the street, are all blasting the news across the entire Internet, including Facebook.

This accusation is ridiculous and unwarranted. It is fake, fake news! The "salacious" purchase is not for a hooker, opioids, videos or even HGH, but for a cane. Of course, this is ludicrous because there is no conceivable way I am even close to being old enough to need such an elderly-type device.

I would like to officially issue a denial to these titillating rumors, but that is difficult to do since TMZ has somehow obtained an invoice addressed to me from a company called "Fashionable Canes" in Largo, Florida. This must be a forgery. (Fake news!) Though I am tempted to claim this cane was for my wife, the Peyton Manning defense on HGH, I won't. Because if my wife found out, I might have to call in medical specialists to extract the alleged cane from an unspecified orifice, and I could end up needing a walker instead of just a cane.

Now you, and the entire world, may be laughing at me, but I assure you the cane, if there really is one, is needed for a medical condition that flares up very infrequently. Let me be clear, even though this ailment is more prevalent in geezers, this does not mean I am old, getting old, or even feeling older. No, this medical condition is just causing me more pain now for some mysterious, unknown reason, that is totally unrelated to my age.

I repeat, it is not due to me being old. The ailment is hereditary. This is all my ancestors' fault. They had the same disorder, but they were highly irresponsible and negligent in dealing with it. Those sheepheads then passed it down to me, and now I have to deal with it by allegedly buying a freakin' cane!

If I had to buy a cane, it would upset me greatly and be a

major blow to my fragile, male ego. It is darn difficult to appear macho, vibrant and relevant when you require the help of a stick to stand upright. (Why not just sit back in this nice recliner, old man?)

This purported cane has not even been used because it has not been needed yet. It might just be available if my ailment flares up. And that is highly unlikely since the illness strikes old people, and I am certainly not that old.

I am sure these scandalous reports come as a shock to my many young, hot female fans, of which there are legions around the world. That's why I am denying this so passionately. I need to assure these women my medical condition only constrains me when I am in the vertical position and in no way limits my ability to perform horizontally. Let me also say that my cane, if it exists, is long and stiff, just like my . . . well you get the idea. Fortunately for me, the cane, unlike other things, does not need 60 minutes and a blue pill to achieve full functionality.

I may no longer be macho, but the rumored cane is distinguished and fashionable. I mean it did allegedly come from a place called Fashionable Canes, didn't it? So, if the women don't find you functional, they should at least find you fashionable (tip of the hat to Red Green).

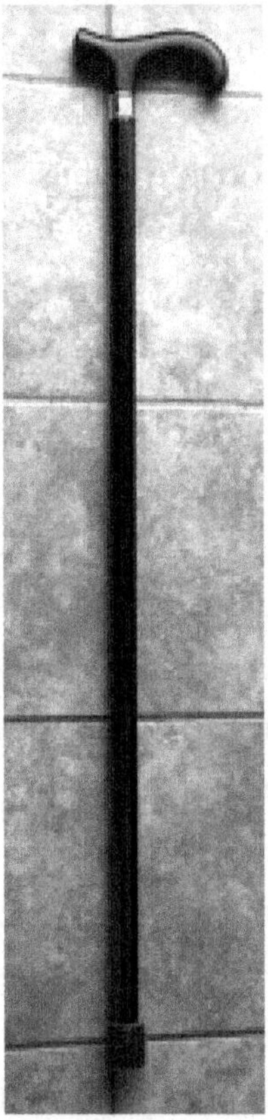

The alleged cane, which I obviously don't need

I would also like to issue a warning to all you insensitive young whippersnappers out there. I am extremely sensitive about having to use this alleged cane in public. If you happen to see me with this device, I strongly suggest against making any mocking-type comments. I swear you may be able to outrun me, but I have a long reach, and if you get within literal striking distance, I will take this cane and smack your freakin' ankle so hard that you won't be able to walk, without, without . . . uh . . . without using a cane. And if you need a recommendation, I may or may not know of a good cane company. If you make the mistake of using the word "cripple", I will take out both ankles Tony Soprano-style.

Now, if I have to defend my honor in this totally justified manner, I will probably fall over. But not like some old guy. No, like a ninja warrior, a master in the art of cane-fu.

Unfortunately, unlike a Weeble, I will not be able to get back up. So, if you see me lying on the ground next to a young guy who is screaming and clutching his ankle, please help me up so I can escape. And do it quickly, since I won't be running away. I will be hobbling using a gosh darn cane. Please do not take any videos or photos at the scene, lest they end up on TMZ and I have to do this pathetic denial thing yet again.

You may think I'm getting cranky, but I'm not. Only old people get cranky. So, I am obviously not cranky, since I am not that old. I am merely just very upset. Upset, not cranky, got it? If you try to argue this point, I will shake my fist at you, sonny boy. And trust me, you don't want that.

This concludes my response to these nasty, offensive, salacious, false, unsubstantiated, malicious, untrue, fabricated, fictional, made-up, fake, unproven, deceitful, rumors and lies. Please carry on with your normal lives and try not to let these awful reports about me disturb you or ruin your day.

Song Explanation:
"Soon I'll be 60 years old
My daddy got 61"

This song creeps me out every time I hear it because very soon I will be 60 years old, and my father died at age 61. No need to remind me of this every time I turn on the radio, Lukas Graham, you stupid sonavabeech.

This concludes The Aging Chronicles (the original subtitle of these posts). I had much more to write on this subject, but for some reason I can't remember any more of it. All this writing has made me very tired, I will be taking a nap now.

The Fat: Fortunately, since posting this in May 2016, I have had to use the cane only one, two-day stretch. However, it is worth having it around just in case.

📖 📖 📖

CHAPTER 6

All About The Homestead

Home and family should be the best things in your life. These stories involve interesting family gatherings, my attempt at beautifying the yard, ornery pets and dangerous yard work. Enjoy!

I Went Hunting In The Bushlands

The Skinny: I am an intelligent, educated man who knows much about many things. However, there are some simple things of which I know nothing about and it is amusing to people when I display this profound ignorance. At least give me some credit for exploring new worlds.

Sometimes men are forced to do things to try to benefit and preserve their marriage. Okay, many times we must do these unpleasant tasks. All right, often marriage can be just doing one uncomfortable thing after another.

Recently, I did something for the first time in my life in an attempt to please my wife. I actually went to a nursery and landscaping store to buy some shrubbery for my wife's birthday. Now you must understand I am not a horticulturalist. I am probably a horti-counterculturalist. I am not interested at all in bushes or shrubs. I don't even notice them unless they grow so much they get in my way or begin to die. At which time I say astute things to my wife such as, "That shrub needs trimmed," or "That bush appears to be dying; maybe you should do something."

What happened that I find myself at the nursery anxiously looking over a vast selection of unknown greenery? Two years ago, the township cleaned out the drainage ditch by our yard for the first time in 19 years. They arrived one day without warning and promptly completed the task. They had the legal right to clear all vegetation within five feet from the ditch to give their equipment proper clearance. They could have easily accessed our ditch by removing just a foot of foliage. Inexplicably, they decided to wipe out the whole five feet.

My wife had spent much time beautifying that part of the yard. It looked lovely, even to a horti-counterculturalist like me. When my wife saw the destruction, she was livid. She wanted to scream at our trustees. Of course, screaming wouldn't bring back any of the plants and such. Being the good husband and the fixer of all catastrophes, I offered to pay for professional landscapers to replenish the area the next spring.

However, my wife didn't take me up on the deal. Probably a combination of principle ("Why should we pay for someone else's stupid behavior?") and personal feelings ("This is my yard and I will deal with it."). However, what remained of the bushes and shrubs after the township massacre did begin to regenerate. Just like when we suffer a setback in life and think the situation will be horrible forever, it does get better over time. In this case, the bank actually started to fill in wonderfully. It looked great, except for two noticeable gaps.

Naturally, men are great for closing gaps. We don't like gaps. Gaps are bad. So, I made the decision to buy my wife some shrubbery for her birthday, and thus, I stood in the middle of this vast selection of foliage with nary a clue as to what I needed. Fortunately, Brad soon appeared to assist me. Brad was a handsome, strapping young lad, and I'm sure the local women enjoyed having Brad tend to their bush and shrub needs. But Brad was not just "beefcake", he was very knowledgeable about his products. Of course, my questions were limited to, "How big does that one get?"

My first choice was a holly-type bush, and Brad suggested I get a male and a female. Apparently, these plants engage in some type of procreating activity. Hubba, hubba! Who knew? I must have missed that lesson in biology class. I have no idea how they mash, but they must do it after dark because I have never, ever, witnessed this hot action and am sure I would remember if I had. So, I got the two holly "love" shrubs and bought a Korean type plant just in case my wife did not like the other selections. You might say I bought the third plant literally "to hedge my bet." Har, har, double har!

However, when I proudly presented the bushes to my wife, she was not pleased. We have our own defined domains in this marriage, and by this purchase, I had crossed over into my wife's landscaping territory. I knew that was a risk, but thought I had the benefit that it was a birthday gift. I was wrong, so wrong, but does that really surprise you?

She looked scornfully at the holly plants and said I wasted my money because she could easily transplant some of the same plants from her mother's yard. I'm thinking, "If this was so easy to do, why wasn't it done at any time in the last two years?" Of course, I don't say this out loud because you don't stay married for 30 plus years by actually saying every thought that comes to mind. Do you?

I had prepared for this outcome, however. I had told Brad that my wife might not like my choices, and he assured me the shrubs could be easily exchanged. I calmly and quietly handed the receipt to my wife and encouraged her to return the bushes and get some better ones.

Secretly, I hoped that she would keep my choices. I had taken the time to think about a meaningful birthday gift, I had driven to the nursery, and I had actually put some effort into my selections. And strangely, I was growing fond (har again!) of the Korean plant. Now there would have been a time that I might not have wanted my wife to interact with that plant-stud Brad, but I wasn't concerned about that now.

I believe after the shock wore off, my wife realized that I had tried to do a good thing, and she decided to plant the bushes. She ignored my advice not to plant the Korean one on the north side of the property. My concern was that a North Korean plot would turn into a communist plant, and I knew from old movies how damaging a communist plant

The Korean plant

could be to your operation. Man, maybe the feds would show up!

After all that, now my wife is very happy. I am very happy. And the bushes appear to be enjoying their new home. I don't know if the male and female have engaged in, well, nature-type activity yet, but I'm sure they will when they get to know each other better and the time is right. Hubba, hubba.

The Fat: I have taken a personal interest in these plants since I took the effort to buy them. I even water them most days in the summer!

His Name Is DAAAAAAAVE!

The Skinny: I posted on Facebook about the weird guy who crashed our annual family reunion picnic. My friend Kori replied that the subject would make a great blog post. I said there wasn't enough material for a whole post. Then Carrie, a family member who wasn't at the picnic because she out of state, took Kori's side and said it would make a terrific post. And they were right!

A group of kinfolk were engaged in a lively conversation at our annual family picnic when we were rudely interrupted by this booming and enthusiastic exclamation: "MY NAME IS DAAAAAAAAAAAVE!" I look over to see a guy in a tank top, long parted '70s-style hair, excessive tats and a large goofy smile, eagerly extending his hand. I shake it and introduce myself, not quite as loudly though.

I had not seen this dude before and I wondered if one of the womenfolk had made a questionable choice of new suitors. Naturally, I am curious about his family ties, but I'm not going to ask him for fear of hearing "MY NAME IS DAAAAAAAAAVE!" again.

He anticipates my question though and says, again hyper-enthusiastically, "I'm not even a member of this family!" Now if I were crashing a not-my-family gathering for, let's say, free beer and food (I can't really blame the guy for grabbing some free appetizers), I might keep it on the down low. I would tell people I was Bill's third cousin, twice removed. But apparently this is not Dave's style.

Dave then became the focal point of our conversation. We engaged in some small (very small) talk during which Dave mentioned that he once knew a woman who had breasts the size of my head. Now I do have a large head, but it needs to be this big to house my large brain, and it is smoothly shaved. But I don't appreciate having it compared to a woman's breast, and frankly, the gleam in Dave's eye when he looked at my head made me very nervous. Creeeeeeepy!

Dave soon scurried over to a new group of people greeting them with another hearty: "MY NAME IS DAAAAAAAAAAAVE!" My cousin confirmed that Dave was indeed crashing the party. He lived in the campground next to the park and the free food and beer was too much of a temptation. He was just like a raccoon but with longer hair. Carrie later informed me via Facebook that Dave had pulled the same stunt last year and labeled him, "The serial, drunk, family reunion, party crasher".

Our conversation was repeatedly interrupted by loud outbursts of "MY NAME IS DAAAAAAAAAAAVE!" as he made it a point to meet everyone at the picnic. I hate to admit it, but

Dave was friendlier to my family than I was!

And Dave has strong networking skills. He really knows how to work a room, or in this case, a picnic. I usually forget people's names ten seconds after being introduced, but not this time! HIS NAME IS DAAAAAAAAAAAVE! You ain't going to forget him! He needs no business card! Because trust me, you're never going to contact him again . . .

However, as I watched him, I realized Dave had violated one important networking rule. He was, as we say in my old neighborhood, $h!+-faced drunk. I would say he had one too many beers, but when the beer is free how can one really determine what is "one too many"? And in this condition, I doubt Dave could count past three.

I couldn't get too upset with ol' Dave though. Sure, he wasn't a family member, but in actuality I was marginally a member of this family. I get to attend on an invitation extended by my second cousin once removed. (Yes, one time he was once removed from a second story window when his girlfriend's husband came home early). But Dave was a friendly guy, and he may not have had a good meal in a while.

But, near the end of the picnic Dave's big moment arrived. For the first time ever, we decided to get a group family photo. Of course, the problem with group photos is the person taking the picture is not included. But now we had a perfect solution! Non-family, party crasher Dave would take the photo. This is going to be so neat!

Dave enthusiastically seized this opportunity. I think he felt some remorse about consuming all the free food and beer. He thought if he was able to help us out and take the photo, then it would be a fair trade, and he would have earned his keep.

We gathered around, happily anticipating this special family moment. No one had to tell us to smile. We were all beaming in the warmth of family love. Dave with a big, goofy smile on his face joyfully aimed his camera phone and shot four pics.

Of course, not one of these photos was legible. They were blurry just like Dave's brain, because Dave was $h!+-faced drunk. So, we all learned a valuable lesson that day: "Never let the most wasted person at your party take the group photograph."

These are truly words to live by. We violated this rule and now we have no group photo, and coincidently, there was no leftover beer.

The Fat: Unfortunately, Dave's attendance at the picnic (turns out someone had invited him) caused a family rift that is still ongoing today. Oh family!

This Essay Is A Pile of Dog Crap

A strange set of circumstances led to an ugly incident at my house last week. My wife was home sick with a nasty virus, I had an early breakfast meeting, and the temperature that morning was a brutal negative 12 degrees.

Usually my wife awakens first, and feeds then walks the dog. I knew the dog would be my responsibility that morning and set the alarm, so I would have enough time to get everything done before leaving for my meeting.

It was past the dog's normal feeding time when I got up. Still, I chose to shower first to keep on the tight schedule. However, after I showered, nature called, and I needed to answer it before my breakfast meeting. Now, while I was tending to my business, the dog burst through the bathroom door and he was not happy. He looked at me as if to say, "My breakfast is late and all you are doing is sitting there reading a magazine and stinking up the house. I'm hungry and I demand some service!"

I finished up, got dressed and hurried downstairs. But I was not greeted by the dog as I expected, but by a pile of dog crap on the floor directly in front of me. It was right in the walkway, presented where I could not miss it.

I was glad the dog crap was on the tile portion of the floor where it could be easily cleaned. My mood changed when I saw a second "gift" about eight feet away on the carpet.

The dog obviously was not happy with my performance that morning. He had sent me a message, actually two messages, to communicate his utter displeasure with my level of customer service. However, as I stared at the crap before me, I realized there were some deeper messages, life lessons if you will:

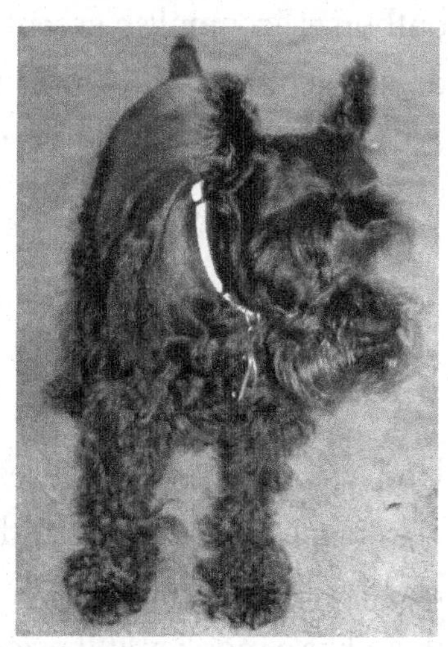
Midnight – Acting as if nothing happened

Life Lesson #1 - Do not put your trivial needs ahead of the more important needs of others.

If you break this rule, there are consequences. The offended party may decide to crap on the floor. At work, they may figuratively crap on your head. Of course it is wrong for them to do this, and they may get the blame. However, you still look bad, and smell bad, and have a pile of crap all over your head. Once the crap is let loose, it is too late. You can't put the toothpaste back in the tube, as it were. Better to make sure other people's needs are attended to, than having to deal with the resulting messy crap.

> **Life Lesson #2** - Do not yell at others when you have contributed to the mess.

I wanted to yell at my dog, but I didn't. Even though he did the crapping, I created the environment to make it possible. I was largely responsible for the crap. I owned some of it (actually technically I owned all of it). How often do we yell at others when we are the ones that help create the mess? What do angry outbursts accomplish except to make others feel as terrible as we do at the moment? My dog had already had a traumatic morning because his routine had been altered. Why should I make it any worse?

> **Life Lesson #3** - When life gives you crap, instead of complaining, figure out the best way to deal with it.

Under normal circumstances it would have been a hassle disposing of the crap. However, there were 16 inches of snow in my backyard. So, I collected all the turds in paper towels and flung them like a monkey at the zoo, far out into the yard. I now realize why the monkeys do this – it is kind of fun!

> **Life Lesson #4** – Even when life gives you crap, find something positive in the pile.

As soon as I heaved the crap into the yard, I had an epiphany. The worst part of my morning would have been walking the dog in frigid, negative 12-degree weather. Because he crapped in the house, I no longer had to do that. I let him out on the deck to whiz and the entire job was complete without me even having to put on a coat! Waking up to dog crap was disturbing, but something positive resulted from it.

> **Life Lesson #5** – Give others credit for wise decisions, even when they cause you some discomfort.

I realized the dog had the choice to poop outside in frigid conditions or inside where it was 82 degrees warmer. Maybe the dog is shrewder than I thought. Well played, I mean, well laid doggy, well laid.

And yes, I extracted all off this from a pile of dog crap . . .

I Am Now Identifying As A Japanese-Mayan

In 2015 a white woman was exposed as pretending to be black. The problem was she happened to be employed as an officer in her local NAACP and a scandal exploded. She claimed there was no issue because although she was white, "she identified as an African-American".

Michael Jackson used to sing "It don't matter if you're black or white". And this should be true in most cases, but not in this one. This woman was in the wrong organization. She meant to join the National Association for the Advancement of White People Who Would Like to Be Black People or NAAWPWWL-BBP for short. But there is no organization like that because even the abbreviation can't fit on a t-shirt.

This issue is literally "black and white" but has become as complicated as all get out. This woman claims she identifies as a black person even though she is white and that makes her black. Now you may scoff at this, but I have some racial identity issues of my own.

I'm Turning Japanese?

Years ago, I received a credit card application encouraging me to "Celebrate (my) Japanese-American Heritage With The Prestige of Visa Platinum." The letter began: "As one who takes great pride in your ancestry, you'll be pleased to know that you can now show that pride with the Japanese-American Heritage Platinum Visa card." A card that "celebrates the pride and traditions of your Japanese-American Heritage". And when I use the card, "I honor my cherished ancestry" (oh boy!).

The card features a map of Japan and an image of Mt. Fuji.

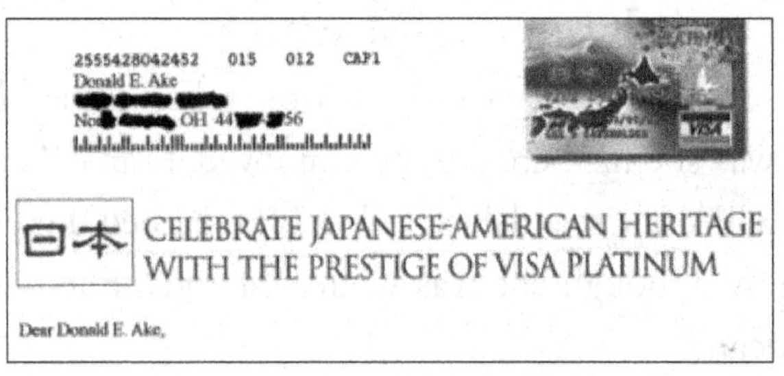

2555428042452 015 012 CAP1
Donald E. Ake

日本 CELEBRATE JAPANESE-AMERICAN HERITAGE
WITH THE PRESTIGE OF VISA PLATINUM

Dear Donald E. Ake,

Apparently, the credit card company did a data sort of three-letter last names that begin and end with vowels, and bingo! I'm Japanese. I showed the letter off at work and my friend Kurt referred to me as Aw-key-sun for the next two weeks and would bow when I passed.

I am the Mayan King

Several years ago, a waiter in Cancun was confused when I handed him my credit card and he saw my name. "You have a Mayan name, but you are not Mayan?" Turns out Ake is a Mayan name, and a royal Mayan name, at that! So I am the Mayan King! "Hakuna Matata" everyone, no need to bow.

But now with all this racial identity stuff in the news I am now ready to embrace my Japanese-Mayan heritage. From now on I will identify as a Japanese Mayan. The Japanese are intelligent, and the Mayans were skilled writers, so you cannot dispute my identity. If you try, you are a bigot in the worst degree. Again, I emphasize, there is no need to bow when we meet.

As a Japanese, I will expect to receive discounts and preferred seating at all hibachi restaurants. As a Mayan, I will expect great sympathy from everyone since my people have perished are without a home. And if there are any hot Mayan chicks out there who are interested in trying to repopulate our race, that's a cause I will enthusiastically support.

We Are Family – I Guess

This blog post is unique because for the first time someone has actually requested that I blog about them. People rarely want this (even if I give them a pseudonym); my former co-worker Erin would often start out his stories with: "Now Don, this is not bloggable".

But my cousin Susan requested that I blog about her (and our family), so I will grant her wish. I'm doing this because Susan is family, and family is very important to me, which is the essence of this post.

I am an only child of an only child. This means not only don't I have any siblings, but there are no aunts, uncles or cousins on my father's side of my family. My mother had three siblings and I do have ten first-cousins. However, that side of the family was never close. I can never remember a time when the cousins were all together. The three cousins I saw most often, abruptly moved to California in the early '70s.

I don't write this to solicit any pity. I married into one of the greatest families imaginable (they are comparable to the Walton's) and my extended family on my father's side includes me in some fantastic get-togethers twice a year (His Name Is DAAAAVE!). No, I tell you this so you can understand how special the following event is. While you may have experienced close family interactions thousands of times in your life, I recently got to experience this myself for the first time in over 40 years.

My cousin Diane was visiting her father in Ohio, and this gave the Roush-family cousins an opportunity for a mini-reunion. Similar to a meeting of mafia clans, all four families were represented. There was Filly Diane (the horse farmer), Patty Ohio (to differentiate from cousin Patty California), The Twins (Susie and Vickie) and Donnie Akron (the city kid).

At this meeting it is "Donnie"; only certain people are permitted to call me Donnie, but this group qualifies. Hey, it's family.

(But for everyone else, MY NAME IS DOOOOOON!)
My cousins communicated as if they had been best friends all their lives. It's like they were speaking their own special language, like it was coded in their DNA. It was amazing to witness. Conversations moved rapidly from topic to topic because it only took a few words to communicate complex thoughts and feelings. These people were completing each other's sentences, not out loud, but in their heads. It was like the words were in a zip file that was exchanged, downloaded and processed instantaneously. Once I learned how to play this game, I joined in and it was a wonderful experience.

Then we sat around and exchanged old, often embarrassing, stories about each other. Several times I felt like a politician saying: "While I do not remember the incident in question, I cannot deny that I may have engaged in the alleged behavior."

While reconnecting with my cousins was a wonderful experience, I'm just not sure I am related to these people at all (even though the AncesteryDNA test claims otherwise.) I see little family resemblance. For example, here are some family traits I identified from this encounter:

Cousins!

1. These People Are Weird

My cousins are a very strange breed. They think weird things, and they make bizarre statements. I mean they are really out there. I'm not talking just standard strange; I'm talking nutsy coo-coo here. They border on insane.

Of course, no one has ever accused me of being that weird, have they? Okay, no one has accused me of being that weird today. Er . . . all right, I guess I may have to concede this one.

2. These People Talk Too Much

My cousins talk a mile a minute. Yap, yap, yap endlessly. You need to listen fast just to keep up. Of course, people never say that about me because I'm usually dominating the conversation... It's a good thing my relatives don't write blogs or they would go on and on about the most mundane things in their lives, expecting people to actually care about their bizarre musings. I can't even image how awful that would be.

3. These People Don't Care What Other People Think Of Them

This is who they are and you better get used to it. It's the attitude of: "You must adapt to me because I'm sure as heck not going to adapt to you". While this sounds very bold, it doesn't get you too far in the business world. I assure you, I possess none of this attitude whatsoever. My failure to reach my career potential was caused totally by wearing the wrong style of underpants all these years.

4. These People Don't Take Life Too Seriously

My cousins have a warped sense of humor. It's twisted, bent and bat- $h!+ crazy. They are a bunch of loons. One photo taken at this gathering features two of my cousins flipping the bird. They are doing it because they are nuts. They are not close to being bad-@$$, they are in fact good-@$$. (Since I am referring to my cousins, it is important to point out I am not using the term "good-@$$" in a West Virginia-type of way). Now you all know this one doesn't apply to me at all. I am serious, reserved and well-refined.

5. These People Have A Superiority Complex

It doesn't matter who you are, what you do, or what you have. I'm sorry, at the end of the day you still are NOT a Roush. We even have a coat of arms. Yes, go ahead and gasp, I am part of a family that possesses a coat of arms! We are Roush and unfortunately you are not. Fortunately, I do not personally have this superiority complex, because let's face it, I'm better than that.

This cousin reunion was the highlight of my summer. It was an incredibly fantastic time. My cousins are great people and I love them dearly, even though I am absolutely nothing like them.

My Shorts Almost Killed Me

The Skinny: This essay is my friend Michael's favorite Ake's Pains post. I had not originally plan to include it in the book. However, Michael protested vehemently, so here it is!

Recently I purchased a pair of "basketball" shorts at my local drugstore. It may seem odd to buy clothing at the drugstore, but they offer "close-out" items at cheap prices. These shorts looked like an excellent bargain at only $3.99!

However, the shorts were powder blue and "silky". Now they weren't exactly "fancy pants". Fancy pants should never ever be worn by guys unless they are working as a clown or golfing. These were more like "snazzy pants". Now snazzy pants are acceptable apparel for younger guys trying to attract young chicks. But my days of trying to attract young chicks are long gone. Snazzy pants are not going to do the trick at my age, and even if they did work, there would be major health risks involved. I'm not referring to having a heart attack, but rather getting killed by my wife. The risk is simply not worth it.

The shorts were a bit too flashy to wear in public (wouldn't want to tempt those young chicks now, would I?). But, I reasoned I could just wear them around the house, and at just $3.99 it was a deal that was just too good to resist.

However, when I tried them on at home, these were in fact "young man pants" and not appropriate for a middle-age body. The shorts were tight in the thighs which meant when I bent over, the shorts quickly slid down about six inches in back. This might be stylish in the 'hood, but not in the 'burbs. If I wore them while picking up branches in the yard, I would be flashing half-moons to the entire neighborhood. This is something no one wants to see, not hot chicks, and especially not the children. Now, the $3.99 price did not look like such a bargain. To get any use out of these things, I decided they would be my designated "lawn-mowing shorts". So, I put on my snazzy, silky pants and fired up my riding mower.

But mowing on a rider often requires you to shift your butt to the high side of the seat on inclines to balance out the weight distribution and prevent the mover from tipping over. However, the first time I shifted my buns to the high side of that seat, gravity and the lack of friction provided by these silky shorts caused my butt to slide violently and unexpectedly to the bottom of the seat.

This happened on a slight incline, so the mower did not tip over. As it were, I let out a loud "Oooooooooweeeeeeeeeeee" and was fortunate not to have slid right off the mower.
Mowing the rest of the lawn was like an amusement park ride; being thrown forcefully to the left and right on inclines and sharp curves, and yelling "Oooooooooweeeeeeeeeeee" repeatedly. I almost went careening off the mower several times. It was as if that leather seat was greased. My butt was sliding all over the place. My booty was out of control like a middle-age woman dancing to rap music at a wedding reception.

I should have known better. It's plain physics. Newton's First Law of Ass-nertia states: A body part in motion tends to remain in motion. And there was no way to stop my large butt once it started to slide in those silky shorts.

If I had flipped the mower over and died, no one would have surmised that it was the stupid shorts that led to my demise. Not even, Sherlock Holmes or The Mentalist. People would have thought I was just careless. It may have even been worse if I had survived. I can imagine young nurses snickering at me as the surgeon worked to reattach my genitals.

"He says he wrecked his mower because he was wearing silky

shorts, tee hee, tee hee, tee hee."

And the Internet headlines would have been just as embarrassing: Man's Snazzy Shorts Nearly Kill Him.

In the words of Dirty Harry: "A man's got to know his limitations." This goes double for middle-age men. And my limitations now include not wearing hip, flashy clothing designed for younger guys. No matter the price, no matter the occasion.

CHAPTER 7

The Blunder Years

I prefer to write about current stories and events. I don't usually enjoy telling old stories from the past, although some do need to be told.

I didn't expect my high school reunion to generate enough material for one essay, let alone the longest chapter in this book. Not to mention, these are also the most personal writings I have ever published.

Every Picture Tells A Story

The Skinny: My 40-year high school reunion generated many old memories even days before the big event. Who would have thought an old photo could say so much?

"When I think back on all the crap I learned in high school – mama don't take my Kodachrome away"– (Paul Simon)

In anticipation of our 40-year high school reunion, Carol thought it would be a swell idea if everyone used their senior yearbook photograph as their profile picture on Facebook. I thought this was an atrocious, massively horrible idea. However, since I was helping organize the reunion, I felt pressured to comply.

It's ironic that high school reunions enable us to relive our high school experience, and now, I was again feeling peer pressure. Wonderful!

I actually liked my photo when it was taken, but over the years I had come to find it rather distasteful. I could never imagine the circumstance that would cause me to ever post this thing on the Internet where millions of people around the world could all simultaneously spit out their respective breakfasts when this hideous image popped up on their screens.

I hoped no one would really do this, but then many new (but really old) profile pics from dozens of classmates started hitting my Facebook feed. Maybe I will not be able to find a photo to post, I reasoned. I wasn't going to search the attic where many copies are buried away somewhere. My best bet was to find the worn, wallet-size one which I had tossed into a folder years ago. I thought it would take some time to search for it, which was fine. I wanted to be able to tell my classmates, "I tried to find the pic, looked everywhere for over 30 minutes, but no luck."

I made a big mistake when I asked my wife for help finding that folder. "Why don't you check the box in the office that has your mother's old stuff in it?" she asked. Three minutes . . . in just three whole minutes, I was holding a 6" x 9" framed copy of the notorious photo. I now remembered this photo was always prominently and proudly displayed in mom's living room next to her favorite chair. The photo most certainly wasn't hideous to her. Instead it was tangible proof that I was cherished. I was her only child, a child she never, ever, thought she would have. The photo was part of her "shrine" to me. So while I disliked seeing that photo each time I visited, it was actually my mother's way of telling me how much she loved me. Why is it that we only understand certain messages until long after the messenger is gone? I carefully removed the photo, scanned it, but I was still hesitant to post it. My wife saw me staring apprehensively at the computer screen, and asked if everything was all right. "Oh, everything is fine," I cautiously responded. Fine until . . . click.

So here's the pic. I thought it might cause somewhat of a reaction on Facebook, but I wasn't ready for what came next. The photo blew up my little section of the Internet. Here, it was even bigger than Kim Kardashian's butt.

Okay, nothing is bigger than that, but you get the idea. Nothing I had posted on Facebook came close to generating this much interest. The final total: 112 "Likes" and 48 comments. Although I doubt all 112 people truly liked the photo. Some of these weren't laughing with me, they were laughing at me.

Of course, a popular topic of conversation was the abundant hair of my youth. People usually don't believe me when I tell them I once had long, flowing hair. Now I have indisputable proof. My Facebook friends pointed out that I had nice tresses. Several people questioned whether I was wearing a wig. Others wondered how it was possible to lose that much hair and still be alive. One guy sarcastically asked how I created the "side poufs". I explained this was accomplished by the use of something called "an electric comb".

The haircut was known as a "Dutch Boy". This style let me grow my hair long without parting it down the middle. My hair does not, oh excuse me, did not naturally part down the middle. And guys in the Kenmore class of 1976 did not use hairspray. If you were ever caught using hairspray, you would have been labeled a sissy, and uh, yeah, the f-word (Not that f-word, the other f-word, the noun). All my college photos show my hair parted down the middle, due to a more refined, accepting environment, and yes, large amounts of hair spray.

I concede the sport coat is butt-ugly by today's standards, but the '70s was a decade of horrible clothes. At one time, I had a pair of cuffed, green plaid pants . . . so hideous. I even wore platform shoes, and at nearly 6'4" the last thing I needed was to be any taller. I still remember banging my head into doorways, hard enough to get woozy, because of those ridiculous shoes. But I wore them anyway because it was the '70s. I only had a couple of sport coats and this was my newest one. It was considered rather snazzy at the time.

However, I was amazed by the tremendously positive response to the pic from the ladies. Apparently, I was a stud back then and didn't even realize it! The younger women liked the pic, the more seasoned ladies like the pic, even some foreign chicks liked it. Yes, all types of women, many of them who are actually "hot", were grooving to that '70s guy.

My former classmate, Mike, claimed that the reason he couldn't get a date in high school was because all the "hotties" were only interested in me. Someone else compared me to Prince . . . Prince Valiant that is. Gail posted, "Kim had the biggest crush on you." That one actually brought a tear to my eye. Kim, who has since passed away, was a sweet, pretty girl, and I had no idea she liked me.

And not only was I a stud, I was also a rock star. Several people asked if I was one of the Beatles. Yes, I was the fifth Beatle, the one who couldn't sing or play guitar. Another person thought I was in the Partridge Family. Yeah, that's it, I was "Donny" Partridge". Unfortunately, I got kicked out of the group after I was caught "practicing" in the back of the band van with Susan Dey. (I thought she loved me ♫.) But by far the strangest comment I received was that I had the Justin Bieber look going on, years before he did. But if that were true, there would have been girls swooning over me in high school, and I'm sure I would have remembered that. If Bieber did steal my look and is now making millions as a result, he will soon hear from my attorney.

The marvelous response on Facebook caused me to take a new look at this photo from a detached, more objective perspective. Well, the kid looks much more handsome than I ever remembered seeing in any mirror. I guess teenage girls aren't the only ones with appearance image issues.

The kid also appears to be very happy, but that is partially an illusion. I was happy, but not that happy. I remembered the photographer being smokin' hot, and when she smiled at me and told me to smile back, well, this is the look you got. You see, some things never change. Booyah!

I also see a young man with tremendous potential, something I never realized at that time. I had a lot more going for me than I ever knew. This lack of confidence did hinder me some, but I have still done very well. No one ever achieves their full potential, but over the last three years I've made up a lot of ground. So, it took the kid a long time, but he finally got there, and getting there is what matters most.

After all those admiring comments from the ladies, I am considering losing 80 pounds and growing my hair out back into that Dutch Boy. I think I'll skip the jacket, though. Shouldn't take me that much time . . .

Nothing More Than Feelings

The Skinny: How long does a high-school crush last? Much longer than I thought. I open up my soul and pour out my feelings in this one.

(Let's start a story on the '70s with some bad '70s music)
Feelings, nothing more than feelings,
Trying to forget my feelings . . . – (Morris Albert)

I was responsible for collecting the reservations for our 40th-year high school reunion. It was exciting to see which classmates were attending when the mail (and email) arrived each day. Some of these people I had not seen since high school. Then one day, a letter arrived that caught my attention. I stared at the return address. "Connie is coming, wow, all the way from Wyoming," I pondered. (name and location changed).

This was somehow significant to me. Connie could be considered a first love, an old flame, or whatever, and I had not seen her in 40 years. As I recorded her reservation, I noted her husband would not be traveling to Ohio, but her sister would be coming with her.

For some inexplicable reason, I kept thinking about Connie and our past relationship over the next several days – not because I still had feelings for her. Obviously, I did not. If I did that would be ridiculous, because it had been 40 years and there is a definite statute of limitations on feelings. So definitely no feelings, no feelings for her whatsoever.

But it did trouble me I couldn't remember how the relationship actually ended. We had kept in contact for a time after graduation. Connie attended a college an hour away, and we exchanged letters, though not love letters, throughout the summer. The romantic interest had faded by that time, but I guess we were both just keeping our options open. However, the letters stopped in the early fall 39 years ago. I didn't know who ended it or why, but I didn't think it was me. Of course, I have no idea why I can remember these old meaningless details when I can't even remember important stuff that happened last week, but it is definitely not because I still have any feelings, because I don't. No, no feelings.

Then surprisingly, the mystery about why the relationship ended was revealed. A couple weeks before the reunion, Stuts (his real name is Tim, but he deserves a cool nickname), had published an e-directory of information he had collected from our classmates. I read that Connie had been married for 39 years. Now I don't need my MBA degree, my keen data analysis skills or even a calculator to figure this one out. Still, I took some solace in the fact I was not rejected, but replaced. This incident turned out to be meaningless because all my other love interests ceased a mere seven months after the letters from Connie stopped when I met my wife-to-be.

As the reunion approached, I felt apprehensive about seeing Connie again. Not because I still had any feelings toward her, because I don't, but because I thought it could be awkward. And

I hate feeling awkward because it's so awkward feeling awkward. It's even awkward for me to write about feeling awkward. In a word, it's awkward.

To handle this anxiety, I told myself the relationship was not substantial, was brief and really hadn't meant anything to me. Maybe we were both just pretending. In actuality, this "thing" wasn't even real. Taking this new perspective helped me calm down and relax.

So, there was absolutely no reason to fear anything about Saturday night. Connie's husband would not be there so there would be no awkward comparisons. Not that I was worried about this, being a noted author and all. And there were no feelings, none at all, hey no worries, no problems.

Still, just to make sure there were no uncomfortable moments, I thought it best to devise a master plan on how I should interact, or avoid interacting, with Connie that evening. Not that I am a control freak or anything resembling a control freak, because I'm not. I just need to be able to carefully manage every situation, so it turns out the way I want, that's all. The plan was necessary to make the evening go smoothly and not because I have any old feelings for her because I don't.

I would greet Connie with the obligatory "It's so great to see you again" and customary hug. I then would say "we'll talk some later" and then excuse myself to greet other new arrivals. After dinner, I would visit Connie's table and engage in a short, polite, conversation, and then quickly disengage. I would not introduce her to my wife because there is absolutely no need for that. Having them converse was one of my worst fears and would cause me extreme anxiety.

The big night arrived, and I was involved in a lively conversation when I glanced over and saw Connie. Our eyes did not meet as much as they locked. I think engineers used this type of human response when they invented missile radar locking systems. My current conversation ended abruptly. I can't remember who I was talking with or what about. Heck, maybe I stopped talking mid-sentence.

I was irresistibly drawn across the room. This is the same concept scientists used when they invented magnetism. No words were spoken before the hug. The hug was surreal. There was no tension. It was unusually relaxed, and it felt totally natural.

Feelings, wo-o-o feelings,
Wo-o-o, feel you again in my arms

Connie seemed delighted to see me. Of course, I was happy to see her, but not that happy because I have no feelings. No feelings, nope, don't feel it.

After the hug, I told her how good it was to see her, and we would talk more later. Just as I expected, more guests arrived, and I promptly excused myself to greet them. I love it when my plans work perfectly. I felt good about things, and even a little smug at this point.

But the evening was about to take a bizarre turn and spiral completely out of control. I was in the back corner of the hall munching on some free appetizers (they were homemade by classmates), talking sports with the husband of a classmate, when I almost choked on my cheese chunk.

In the far opposite corner of the hall, all by themselves, I saw my wife and Connie engaged in conversation. How was this even possible? As planned, I had not even introduced them earlier, but they had apparently met on their own and were talking up a storm. My superb plan had started to unravel like an old sweater. "What could they be talking about?" I wondered. My first inclination was to sprint over there and put a stop to this. Then I realized they might be talking about me. That possibility made me consider running swiftly out the back door and never looking back.

And it wasn't polite, "I just met you" conversation, either. They were laughing and chatting just like they had been best friends for years. Again, how is this even possible? They just met and they have nothing, absolutely nothing, in common, right? Oh — oh, oh, ohhhhhhh. Okay, so apparently, I have a "type", not a physical "type" but a personality type, and these kindred personalities had become fast friends. I would strongly have denied I had a "type" before that evening. But now it appears that obviously, I do, and I never deny things that are obvious.

It was impossible for me to concentrate on my conversation with this disaster occurring directly in my line of sight. I kept glancing over every ten seconds or so, hoping desperately that Connie and my wife would just stop yacking away. Finally, after what seemed liked hours to me, they parted.

However, minutes later, as I continued to hobnob with my classmates, I noticed my wife quickly walking toward me with a big smile on her face. She obviously had something important to tell me, but what could it be?

"Good news, Connie and her sister are going to sit with us!" she exclaimed. I faked a broad smile and proclaimed. "That's great!" I then tried to return to the festivities unrattled.

Great, that is just great. Really, really, great. I was perplexed that my wife was so happy her new "best friend" was going to sit with us. But now, my seemingly perfect plan was holding together as well as a seeding dandelion in a tornado. I began to experience a panic attack. My pulse quickened. My breathing intensified. My blood pressure was rising. I attempted self-talk to calm down. "It's going to be okay. You can do this. Everything will be fine," I told myself. And that worked. The panic attack stopped, for about 30 seconds, until I remembered:

The joke, the joke, THE JOKE!!!!!!!!!!!!!!!!!!!!!!!!!!!

After dinner, Stuts and I were doing a short comedy routine (with me wearing a hippie wig). We would present some interesting facts about our classmates (from Stuts' e-directory) and then make some funny quips about them. Stuts had insisted we include that Connie now lived in Middle-of-Nowhere, Wyoming, to the skit. The best joke I could come up with went like this:

Stuts: "Connie lives on a ranch in some place called Middle-of-Nowhere, Wyoming, and rides horses every day.

Me: You know, I really liked her in high school. In fact, I planned to marry her.

Stuts: Well that explains it!

Me: Explains what?

Stuts: She obviously moved to Wyoming, so you couldn't find her, and those horses are there for a fast getaway in case you ever did!

There was no way, absolutely no way, to tell that joke with my wife and Connie seated a few feet from each other. I already knew the joke could upset my wife, but was willing to take that risk. The joke could also embarrass Connie, but I never anticipated her sitting at my table. This had the potential for a huge disaster. My master plan now was at risk of a nuclear explosion. Fortunately, I had control of the detonator.

As a more intensified panic attack began, I needed to find Stuts right away and get that joke removed from the routine!

This was part one of a two-part post, so I ended with a teaser:

- Will Don be stupid enough to actually tell that joke?
- What is going to happen at that table during dinner?
- What 40-year old secret will be revealed?

In a crazed panic, I rush over and tell Stuts we have to pull "The Joke" from the routine and why. I'm so flustered, I'm not sure I'm even making sense. Stuts has been a good friend since grade school, and he knows me very well. He is initially amused by my concern and assumes I am joking.

Stuts (grinning widely): Well, you weren't serious about wanting to marry Connie. You made that part up, right?

Me: *(With a wide-eyed, panicked, face and slowly nod my head)*

Stuts (Still smiling): Yeah, but it's still okay. I mean, she's not hot, is she?

(Conveniently Connie was standing at the next table over)

Me: *(Motioned with my head for him to judge for himself, panicked face still in place)*

Stuts *(No longer smiling, deadly serious expression)*: Oh $h!t! What are you going to do?

But Stuts was not really asking me for a decision. When a guy in the Kenmore Class of 1976 asks you that question, with that expression, in that tone, he is challenging you to be a man and not a wuss. This is how we developed our manhood in high school – it was how we learned to become men.

Of course, the wise decision was to not tell "The Joke". There was no question it needed to be cut from the routine. I have had 40 years to define and develop my manhood and I am very secure in my masculinity, so there was really no need to ask that question. However, we were at the high school reunion and we were reliving our high school days, and Stuts had just challenged my manhood.

My fearful expression transformed into something resembling a Dirty Harry scowl. My chin jutted out and my chest puffed as I gritted my teeth. I pointed a finger at Stuts and said with bravado, "We are doing that joke and I will deal with any consequences." With that I spun and marched away confidently. I had only taken a few steps when suddenly my logic returned. Deal with the consequences? How are you going to deal with those consequences? What the heck are you thinking?

I made the pre-dinner announcements and gave the prayer. I prayed for my classmates, I prayed for the meal, and secretly I was praying to still be alive at the end of the evening. I then retreated to my place at the table seated right between Connie and my wife. Connie and I at once started talking. We didn't have to catch up on a lot of life events since being Facebook friends keeps you informed. I'm not even sure what we talked about. It was one of those times that what you talk about is not nearly as interesting as who you're talking with. Like when you are young and in … oh. Please forget I even mentioned that.

If high school reunions are supposed to take you back to the past, Connie and I travelled quickly back in time. The conversation was mesmerizing as if we were the only two people in that crowed room. Which, of course, is odd since my wife was right there. Connie and I both leaned in towards each other, but that's only because the room was very noisy. I'm sure if an expert in body language observed us, he would have obviously come to the wrong conclusion. Because I have no feelings, no feelings, none whatsoever. And I was sure Connie had no feelings either.

Dinner ended, and it was "show time". It did feel a bit strange combing out that long wig and primping in the men's room. Fortunately, only one guy entered while I was posing in the mirror and for some reason he left rather quickly.

The routine was going great and we were getting lots of laughs. We were nearing the end and "The Joke" was coming up. As Stuts started "The Joke", I took a deep breath, there was an adrenaline rush, and it seemed like we were speaking in slow motion. Stuts perfectly delivered the punch line, I acted offended– and the audience broke out in raucous laughter.

Me and Stuts captivating the crowd

Personally, I don't find a joke about a woman moving thousands of miles away to avoid me as being very funny, but the crowd sure loved it. And incredibly, the person who laughed the loudest was my wife. It was so loud in fact, I could discern her laugh above all the others. While I was very relieved "The Joke" had not upset my wife, I was a bit offended she found this joke so freakin' funny. I started to worry that Connie might have a guest room on the ranch, and maybe even an extra horse.

The routine ended, and I returned to my seat. Connie complimented me on the performance, so I knew she was not embarrassed. Things were good! I had survived in a Gloria Gaynor-type way, but the night was not over.

A few minutes later, David visited our table and wondered how I had the guts to tell that joke with my wife in the audience. Before I could answer, my wife jumped in to defend me. This seldom happens because most of my inane comments are indefensible. But hey, this time it was a funny joke at my expense, which featured her new best friend Connie. So, what's not to like?

I then told David that Stuts thought the part about me wanting to marry Connie was not true when it really was. As I said this, I caught a glimpse of someone on my left, nodding. I turned and saw Connie. In the excitement of the moment, I had forgotten she was still sitting there. And, she was beaming, almost glowing. It's difficult for a man to spark that type of response in a woman, especially a middle-age woman. What had I done to elicit this response?

This was much too complicated to figure out at that moment, but my best "post-game" analysis is this:

Our relationship in high school was typical of "first loves". It was bumpy, awkward, muddled, frustrating and painful. I was horrible at this game, and Connie while better at it, was not good enough to make up for my deficiencies. As a nervous, insecure, self-conscience 17-year-old, I could never express my true feelings to her. And as a blossoming young woman in an early relationship, she needed to hear those words. She needed this affirmation from me and, sadly, it never came.

Until I delivered it just a few minutes ago, albeit 40 years too late. It didn't matter that I was wearing a stupid wig. It didn't matter that it was part of a joke. No, I had spoken the words and they were true. And she knew they were true and that's all that mattered. And better yet, they were proclaimed on stage into a microphone to a hundred of our peers, no less. Sometimes a message delivered late, even years late, still brings joy to the recipient. Those words were special, special enough to produce a glow. (If you are keeping score: I thought "The Joke" would upset my wife and embarrass Connie. The result was my wife found it hilarious and Connie felt honored. My ability to understand women and anticipate their reactions is astounding. And as you can see, it hasn't improved much in 40 years.)

After David left, it was just Connie and I at that round table, seated semi-across from each other, similar to a heads-up poker match. I looked at Connie and our eyes locked on for the second time that evening. She was no longer beaming, but there was a light burning in those eyes. At that moment, I realized that she had brought some old feelings with her to the reunion that night, which I found odd, because I have no feelings. Why would I have any feelings whatsoever?

I stared at Connie with my best poker face. A face that said, "I have no feelings now and I had no feelings then, absolutely none. I am so totally devoid of any feelings that I'm numb. My whole body is numb. I'm so numb, even my skull is numb. Please believe me, don't call my bluff. Do not call my bluff."

Well, it's no surprise the women who know you best can read you well. She was not fazed by my façade. She indeed called my bluff by raising the stakes and giving me "The Look". Back in high school, I was powerless to resist "The Look". It was that look that always made me melt. It was "The Look" that kept me coming back to her even when I wanted to stay away. And now I was face-to-face with "The Look", albeit with a few wrinkles, once again.

My plan for the evening was to conceal any feelings that I might still have. Connie had already revealed her feelings, and now her goal was to entice me to express mine. She had put my great master plan to the ultimate test.

But since high school, I have grown into a very manly man, a man with great resolve and tremendous inner strength. A man who could easily pass this acid test without even blinking.

Okay, so I failed a little, in the same sense that the Cleveland Browns failed to win the Super Bowl this year. If I were an iceberg, the hall would have been flooded, so maybe a feeling or two leaked out.

Now after all these years, all the cards were finally on the table. It was intriguing that so much had been expressed by two people without a word being spoken. I guess this is how wild animals communicate, right before they --- well, that is not going to happen here. If it had, do you really think I would be writing about it? This ain't no made-for-TV-movie.

The next day I realized something important. I had always

viewed "The Look" as something Connie did to manipulate and control me, and I had resented her for that. I now realized "The Look" was her positive, primal reaction to me. It was a natural response she had no control over.

If I had done the right things, said the right things, and acted more like a man than a boy back in the day, this courtship could have turned out much differently. For 40 years, I had felt like a loser regarding this relationship, but now I know this was not the case. I had not lost; I was a winner who failed to claim the prize.

There is a huge difference.

But, I have no regrets unless I can regret ever being 17 years old. And that, of course, is fruitless because the only way from 16 to 18 is by Route 17, even if it is a bumpy road.

And in no sense, is Connie "the one that got away". There is no "one that got away" if you are happy with "the one you caught". The best part of this story is that Connie found a husband much better for her, and my wife is a superior match for me. Therefore, life has turned out so grand for both of us. No, Connie's not "the one that got away", but she is "the one who could have been".

At the end of the night, there was a long goodbye, but there was nothing salacious or prurient about anything that happened that evening. Just a couple of old friends, expressing some old feelings, resolving some old issues. There was no heat in this old flame.

Still, it's probably a good thing Connie lives in Middle-of-Nowhere, Wyoming. I'm just sayin'.

The Fat: After I finished writing this, I found out psychologists have determined that "first loves" can remain stuck in your brain forever. This made me better about the whole night. I'm not weird, I'm normal! Okay, I'm still weird.

You Know I Won't Dance

The Skinny: This has nothing to do with the reunion, but it is a humorous story from my senior year in high school, so I included it in this chapter.

You know I can't dance, you know I can't dance (Leo Sayer)

(As always, names have been changed to protect everyone of everything.)

The announcement that tickets were available for the 1976 Kenmore High School Senior Prom created quite a buzz at the school. The event was much more important to the girls than the guys. To senior girls, it was the social event of the year and it was essential to be there to maintain your social status. To most of the guys, it was just another dance. Now if you had a girlfriend, you had to go. If you were unattached, you might invite a girl hoping to spark a new relationship. But otherwise, the boys were not too into it.

Almost immediately, "The Question" was asked of me:

"Don, are you going to the senior prom?"

This event involves slow dancing, wearing fancy-smancy clothing, and being serious and refined for an extended amount of time. I abhor all of these things (my lack of dancing skills has been previously detailed) and I didn't have a girlfriend (things had cooled with Connie by this time), so I had no reason or desire to attend, none whatsoever.

Now when a guy asked me "The Question", he wanted the assurance it was acceptable not to attend. But if all his friends were going, he didn't want to be left out. I never asked this question of anyone because I wasn't going to this stupid prom, regardless.

When girls asked me "The Question", I thought they might be fishing for an invitation or just curious, because the event was so important to them. But after repeated inquiries, I wondered if there could be a craftier, even sinister motive. I couldn't prove it, but I suspected somewhere in Cindy Nolan's basement was a blackboard with the names of senior girls needing dates on the left and uncommitted senior boys on the right. A team of girls would then meet in secret to share information on how to pair couples up. It was a primitive form of Match.com. It was similar to the NFL draft: With the third pick in the 1976 Kenmore High, Senior Prom Draft, Becky Hollins selects Troy Maynard! Once the names were matched up, they launched their diabolical plan. One day after Physics class my friend Janet asked me "The Question", but with an added twist:

Janet: Are you going to the prom?

Me: No, I'm not.

Janet: Well, I just wanted to let you know that
Rhonda Sandling wants to go with you.

Me: (looking perplexed) Thanks for letting me know.

It was no surprise Rhonda Sandling wanted me for her prom date. Rhonda had a huge crush on me and had been trying to spur my interest for months. Rhonda was pretty, tall, and pleasant. We may have made a great couple. But Rhonda came on way too strong, stronger than your Aunt Gertrude's perfume strong. She made no secret she wanted to marry me and have my babies, and maybe not in that order.

Rhonda scared the heck out of me. I was only 18 and not ready to make any babies. I needed the opportunity to get to know her, woo her, and then see where it led. If I took her to the prom, I feared she would misinterpret my intentions. It would be a magical, special night for her, too special. This action might commit me to a relationship for the entire summer. If I couldn't extract myself from her clutches, or if babies happened, we would be making wedding plans in the fall. In my mind, asking her to the prom could be equal to a wedding proposal, so I couldn't take that risk.

There was now a highly organized campaign directed at me by the senior girls. But, there was absolutely no way I was going to the prom, NO WAY. However, I had greatly underestimated the strength and commitment of my adversary.

The entire time, different senior girls were asking me "The Question" and kept tightening the screws:

Random Senior Girl: Are you going to the prom?

Me: No

RSG: Well, Rhonda Sandling really wants to go with you.

Me: Thanks for letting me know.

Then they added the sad look of disappointment when I didn't show interest. A look that said: You are a mean, horrible jerk if you don't take Rhonda to the prom when she wants to go with you soooooooo much. You are a disgusting piece of crap.

Worse yet, they were successfully picking off my fellow prom holdouts one by one. Troy Maynard did ask Becky Hollins to the prom. Phil Cooper invited his designated date, Ann Nichols. These victories must have emboldened them to turn the heat up on me.

Indeed, I was weakening, and they could smell blood. On Friday, I got "The Question" in the morning, and then they hit me again in the afternoon; a cute cheerleader delivering the inquiry with a very convincing sad look of disappointment. I was now upsetting cute cheerleaders with my decision. When the final bell rang, I rushed to my locker, grabbed my stuff, and sprinted out the door.

I was still upset that evening and I couldn't stop thinking about the prom problem. At that moment, I realized I had lost this battle. Unbelievably, I would have to attend the senior prom. The pressure was just too much for me to bear.

But maybe I didn't have to take Rhonda. If I'm going to surrender, could I do it on my own terms? If I could find another date, the questioning would stop. If I couldn't, I would be taking Rhonda and her risks to the prom.

Unfortunately, by this time, my options were limited. All the senior girls I had interest in already had dates. I could take a non--senior, but that would draw the heated wrath of every senior girl in the school.

I considered inviting Barb. She had asked me "The Question" a couple times, and she appeared to signal her availability when I didn't show any interest in taking Rhonda. However, there were issues here also. Barb was very short and had huge bazoombas.

Matched against my height, we might inadvertently engage in "dirty dancing" at the prom.

And she was overweight, a shallow reason to reject her. I was afraid guys like Walt and Keith would ridicule me if I took "the fat girl" to the prom. This fear seems so ridiculous now. Walt and Keith were losers then and they are still losers now. Why would I respect their opinion at all? I believe I would have had the best time at the prom with Barb, even with no dirty dancing.

Then I came up with a totally illogical, bizarre, thinking-outside-the-box choice: Sarah Edwards. I reasoned that Sarah Edwards might still be available because she had a physical abnormality.

I know what you're thinking: "Ahh Don, this is going to be a very heartwarming story about how you took the ugly girl with the cleft palate to the prom; no one else would and you gave her a precious, lifetime memory. That is so sweet, and you are such an awesome person." But of course, you would be wrong, so, so, wrong.

Sarah Edwards' physical abnormality was that she was stunningly beautiful, drop-dead gorgeous. Excuse my sexist, blatant heterosexual description, but she was 5' 11" of curvaceous excellence topped off with striking features and flowing, fiery red hair. If she were a road, she would be lined with "Dangerous Curves Ahead" signs. She was also intelligent, talented and dignified. This was not just my opinion, Sarah had won the regional beauty pageant and would soon compete for the state crown.

I knew Sarah from the newspaper staff. We would occasionally talk, but she was more of an acquaintance than a friend. No guy at our school was worthy of dating her. Because her family was moving to Puerto Rico that summer, I assumed she didn't have a boyfriend at another school either.

And she had not talked about going to the prom during newspaper meetings. The senior girls had no doubt left her name off their board because they figured the beauty queen needed no help getting a date. But she did because all the guys were intimidated by her. Sarah was very tall, and not a frail, skinny girl. She had filled out perfectly into a desirous creature; she was a woman among girls. However, her size did not intimidate me. At nearly 6'-4" I could look her in the eye (those beautiful blue eyes), provided I could keep my eyes off the rest of her.

But it was a totally ludicrous idea to even think about asking her to the prom. This would be a futile, and possibly embarrassing, effort. This option was outrageous, insane and had little chance of success. It would have been literally laughable if I had shared it with my friends, which is of course why I didn't. It was just plain silly.

I was under extreme pressure and not thinking rationally. I reasoned that Sarah was a good option because losing out to a beauty queen would not embarrass Rhonda. Also, if Sarah Edwards somehow fell for me, she was moving to Puerto Rico. So, a breakup would be easy. (I said I wasn't thinking rationally, right?)

As hare-brained as this decision was, Sunday night I developed my plan for asking Sarah to the prom on Monday. No guy at the school had the guts to ask Sarah Edwards to the prom, but that was soon about to change.

This was the end of Part 1 and I again included teaser questions:

- Who will Don end up taking to the prom?
- Will Sarah Edwards laugh in Don's face?
- Will Don end up engaged to Rhonda? (Were there babies involved?)
- What prom night incident gets Don in trouble eight years later?

Part 2 was titled: I Fooled Around And Fell In Love Ah, but since I met you baby, love's got a hold on me I fooled around and fell in love – (Elvin Bishop)

Asking Sarah Edwards to the prom is one of the craziest decisions I have ever made, but I was desperate and out of my mind. This had little chance of success, but for personal satisfaction it had to be done. My plan was that after Sarah declines my offer, I would then ask Rhonda. Yes, I would have lost, but at least I would have tried to avoid it. When I'm standing at the altar and Rhonda starts walking down the aisle, I will be thinking, "If only Sarah Edwards would have gone to the prom with me, I wouldn't be in this mess. This is all Sarah's fault, not mine."

Monday after the newspaper staff meeting, I followed Sarah to her locker. I was only mildly nervous, because I fully expected to be rejected. It was just a matter of how and when. I envisioned she would first be a bit startled when I approached her, then slightly amused after I issued the invitation. She would then say she wanted to check her schedule or some other excuse, and would graciously decline my offer on Tuesday. I wasn't overly concerned if the rejection became public knowledge. It would not be that embarrassing to be rebuffed by Sarah Edwards. The worst-case scenario would be if she laughed in my face, "You silly little boy! Go ask Rhonda like you're supposed to and leave me alone." I hoped she was too classy to do that.

I acted like a worthy suitor and approached her confidently. I looked into her eyes with my best, "Oh baby, you know you want it look," and delivered the invitation flawlessly, with no hint of fear.

I immediately knew something was amiss. She smiled subtlety at me and seemed amused, almost pleased, at my request. I studied her face intently for her next response.

Then her large, gorgeous blue eyes widened.

(My pulse quickens)
Her luscious lips turn from a grin to a full smile.

(My adrenaline starts to flow)

"Sure, it would be great to go with you!" Sarah gushed.

(I pretend that was the answer I had expected.)

"That's wonderful! We will discuss the details later," I exclaim as I flash my signature big, fake smile.

I turn quickly to leave, not only because of what just happened, but my next class was one floor up on the opposite end of the building. I take two steps, and then I fully realize what just happened. The left side of my brain screams out to the right:

"YOU DO REALIZE WE ARE TAKING SARAH EDWARDS TO THE PROM?"

At this realization, I become literally weak in the knees (this has only happened a couple times in my entire life). Now it would be a travesty to collapse in the hall right after such a manly display of bravado. Somehow, with no feeling in my knees, I am able to walk five more steps and duck around the corner to the left of the stairwell.

I lean hard against the brick wall for support and begin to hyperventilate. I wait a few moments because I can't even climb the steps in this condition. My knees recover, my breathing slows, and I rush to class beating the bell by seconds. But I'm sure I didn't hear a single word that teacher said the entire period.

Of all possible scenarios, I had never prepared for this one. Two weeks ago, I was dead set against even going to the prom, now I was taking Sarah Edwards, go freakin' figure.

Most guys who scored this coup would have broadcast it at once to everyone at the school. "Who has two thumbs and is taking Sarah Evans to the Prom? This Guy!" "Oh yeah Tom, I guess taking a cheerleader to the prom is kind of nice. I happen to be taking a beauty queen."

But I respond like a jewel thief who had pulled off the heist of the century. I don't tell a soul because I'm still in shock. The only person I ever told about my prom date without being asked was my mother, and that was only because I needed the cash.

But the following morning, the rumor was spreading like wildfire throughout the school. I was pleased that Sarah had told her friends. I was worried she might be too embarrassed to reveal her date. And, it was only considered a rumor at first because few people actually believed it.

I spent the entire day confirming the news. The girls would

say, "I heard you are taking Sarah Edward to the prom." (Meaning "is it true?) I would answer. They would say "that's great" and then smile. All this sudden female attention was great, really great.

Now the guys would approach me with an expression of skepticism and bluntly ask, "Are you taking Sarah Edwards to the prom?" When I said "yes", they would say "Wow!" (with an expression on their face that said: "I didn't know you had the balls to do that!").

Yes, suddenly I was a stud muffin, a big man on campus, and I had big balls. With apologies to Dr. Seuss: "And what happened then? Well, at Kenmore they say, that Don's small balls grew three sizes that day."

Surprisingly, now I was enjoying my new notoriety. People were showing more interest in me and giving me more respect. I now started to strut down the halls with a new manly gait, although with my hips set wider to make room for my bigger, well, you get the idea.

My strategy for prom night was simple: Don't do anything to mess things up. Make no mistakes.

I never wanted to go to prom in the first place, but dating Sarah Edwards made things much more interesting. I commandeered my father's Ford Galaxy 500. The car is so big it could be a limo. I hoped I could keep my composure in this high-pressure situation.

My fortitude was tested when I picked up Sarah. She was wearing a light-blue, stretchy, clingy dress that held tightly to every beautiful curve of her body. There was nothing immodest about it, except that body poured into that dress, oh my. Oh, my, my, my! (Excuse me, I still get the vapors thinking about it). And she was even more imposing in her high heels, which she could wear because her date (that would be me) was so tall.

It was like a grand entrance when we arrived at the hall. The noise level literally dropped as people stared. I relished this, even though all the attention was focused on the eye-candy on my arm. It didn't matter how much the other girls spent on their dresses, hair or primping, none could match Sarah's awesomeness that night. She was so radiant I felt I should be wearing white gloves like the guy in charge of escorting the Stanley Cup.

The evening was nice. No big mistakes were made . . . until I was by the punch bowl when they sloshed in a large refill. Not the place to be when wearing a white jacket.

I didn't make a fool of myself on the dance floor, and I even let a couple guys dance with Sarah which just added to my stature. "You want to dance with my date, fine. No, sorry, I really don't want to dance with yours."

I only made one request of Sarah the entire night. It was announced that professional photographs of the couples could be purchased for $25. Oh, I wanted a photo of this. I wanted it more than I have ever wanted a photo in my life. (Okay, it's my duty as a husband to claim I really wanted my wedding photos more, but you be the judge.) At that moment I was so psyched I couldn't even ask her. I stared at her with the best "begging" face I had. She looked at me and asked, "Do you want a photo?" I quickly and enthusiastically nodded. I do have a huge smile on my face in the photo, and let me assure you, there was nothing fake about it. It was the best $25 I have ever spent in my life.

It was an enjoyable evening. I was glad I went, which is surprising considering my prior attitude. I took Sarah home and received an obligatory "friend kiss" – slight lip contact. There's been more passion when kissing my cousins. Ah, wait, that came out wrong. Hey, I live in Ohio, Northern Ohio! Let's just forget I even mentioned it.

In the days after prom, I couldn't stop thinking about Sarah Edwards. Being with Sarah Edwards had made me popular. Sarah Edwards went to the prom with me. I liked having Sarah Edwards on my arm. I looked and felt very manly when I was with Sarah Edwards. Sarah Edwards is stunningly beautiful and nice and tall and a redhead and, and, and (well ladies you know what happens next, you guys not so much).

Yes, I fell in love with Sarah Edwards. As irrational as it was for me to ask her to the prom, it was even more irrational for me to fall in love with her. Of course, falling in love is not rational. If it were, the human race would have ended a long time ago.

In actuality, I didn't really fall in love with the "person" Sarah, just the image of Sarah. We had nothing in common. I mean she didn't even like football for Pete's sake. This was a poor match, but when you are young your emotions (and hormones) can spin out of control like a hurricane.

A few days later, I saw Sarah at a school-sponsored, senior class party. I swaggered up to her exuding an attitude that said, "Hey Baby, remember me? We had those magical moments at the prom." But Sarah treated me like a, like a, friend, a mere acquaintance. How could she? I was crushed. My true love, my soul mate, was spurning me and moving to Puerto Rico where I might never see her again.

Lest you think those emotions were not real, it took me two

weeks to recover, hormones and teen emotions being what they are. I did manage to get her a copy of the photo before she left. And then she moved to Puerto Rico with her splendid blue dress, and I never heard from her ever again.

Now if you are keeping score, and I hope you're not, my first love moved to Middle-of Nowhere, Wyoming, after our relationship ended and my prom date moved all the way to Puerto Rico. At least neither of them became a nun.

One More Prom Story

Eight years after the prom, Bob (yes, that friend Bob, the one who often causes me problems) and his wife Diane, came over to our newly purchased first home for dinner. Afterward, the conversation turned to our high school days. Bob and I graduated in the same class, and Diane graduated from the same school, three years later. My wife (who is not Rhonda) attended a different school. I have no idea how the subject of senior prom ever came up.

Bob: (to me) Did you go the senior prom?
Me: Yes, I did.
Bob: You did? Who did you take?
Me: Sarah Edwards.
Bob: (with a scornful look of disbelief) You did NOT take Sarah Edwards to the prom!
Me: Yes, I did.
Diane: (laughing – I told you it was laughable) You, most certainly did NOT ever take Sarah Edwards to the prom!

I know it was silly to argue about something that happened eight years ago and at first, I didn't care if they believed me or not. But now I had a woman laughing at me, and my wife was wondering why I was lying about my prom date and upsetting our guests.

Finally, I had enough of this ridicule. I scurried upstairs and quickly found the prom photo (easy to locate because we had just moved in) and triumphantly presented it to Bob and Diane. There was stunned silence. Bob raises his head and gives me that same look of admiration from eight years ago. Finally, he mutters out a comment, "Yeah, that's Sarah Edwards." Diane just stares down at the photo in total disbelief. She can't say a word. Eight years later, and people are still stunned by my prom date!

Bob hands back the photo and, of course, my wife wants to see it. I give it to her, but I fail to see her reaction because I am too focused on gloating over proving that I did indeed take a beauty queen to the prom. We talk for a while longer, and then Bob and Diane depart.

Now, my wife is not the jealous type. She has only expressed jealousy a few times during our many years together, and on most of those occasions, believe it or not, I have been totally innocent. But when she gets jealous, she expresses her displeasure in a very passionate way, very passionate, as a tornado is passionate. I don't know if it was because I found the photo so quickly. I don't know if it was the awesomeness of Sarah Edwards in that tight blue dress. I don't know if it was my huge, intense smile in the photo. But Bob and Diane weren't out of my driveway five seconds when my wife expresses her intense reaction to that photograph. Thanks, Bob. Thanks so much for bringing this up, you stupid sonavabeech.

Now, I know you really want to see that photo of me, and especially Sarah Edwards poured into that clingy, blue dress. But that photo is now buried somewhere deep in the attic, and I would need my wife's help to find it. So, you will not see that photo, and I will continue to live.

The Fat: I think we are all glad we only had to go through high school once.

📖 📖 📖

CHAPTER 8

Marital Blissness

I believe the interaction between women and men, as we try to keep the planet populated, is the most humorous thing about life. The two genders are so different but are continually brought together by the bond of sexual attraction.

Please remember I am writing about these differences between men and women from a middle-age guy's perspective. I try to be as fair as my testosterone will let me!

Here we have essays about unrealistic marriage expectations, relationship boundaries and compromising positions. Enjoy!

Women Go "Nuts" Over Me

The first thing I noticed after finding my seat were the three stunningly beautiful flight attendants on the plane. I checked my calendar to make sure it was still 2015 and not the 1980s.

For those who are too young to remember the '80s, all stewardesses, as they were previously called, were young and babe-licious. In fact, it was a requirement for the job. But after job discrimination laws came into play, the airlines had to change their policy.

In response, first they hired attractive older women. Then it was any woman, and then males, and finally even men. Now, anything goes.

Earlier this year, I encountered the largest flight attendant ever. She was a big woman, large might even be a more appropriate term! (As a matter of fact, she could have been one of the Butt Sisters). She was so large, she had problems moving through the aisle sideways. If there was an emergency that required me to slide past her to make it to safety, I was going to die. She had a backside that Sir Mix-A-Lot would enjoy, and I got to experience it up close and personal when she leaned over to talk with someone across the aisle. If this encounter had happened in another venue, I would be slipping her a dollar bill.

But this flight was going to be different. Three outstanding babes made up the flight attendant team! Whoaaaa Nelly! Turn those air vents wide open because it's getting hot in here! Wooohooo, sis boom bah, schwing, homina, homina, oh baby! Blonde, brunette and raven-haired beauties; it's a trifecta baby!

However, there would be no flirting with these young women, there would be no ogling, and there would be no leering or staring. I would be careful to not even make eye contact. I would be on my best behavior (Yes, I have a best behavior; it's not that good, but it's the best I got). Because in this case, this wasn't a business trip. I was on vacation, and my lovely wife was seated next to me.

Now I wasn't even tempted to flirt with them. It's just not in my nature to act that way. I am a male of the new millennium. I find this behavior unacceptable, unprofessional, and demeaning to women. That's why I have never engaged in this conduct either personally or in my entire business career.

Okay, unless the woman was smoking hot, then maybe some . . . Uh, okay maybe if she was just fairly attractive, just a little . . .

But if I did flirt, let me assure you that it was classy and very respectful to the women involved. And if you don't believe me, just ask any woman that I have ever worked with. (Jennifer and Jan: If you are reading this and someone actually asks you about this, it would be great if you could just deny ever knowing me, okay Honeycakes?)

Everything on the flight was going great until it was time for the three babes to pass out the snacks, bags of peanuts and pretzels. I was seated in the middle of the plane right where the ladies had divided up the sections for snack distribution. Finally, it was my turn for snacks. The blonde babe looked at me apologetically and explained she had run out of pretzels, and asked if I would like two bags of peanuts instead. I smiled and nodded. I was famished, and the peanuts are more filling.

When she saw that I preferred the peanuts, she playfully tossed me two more bags. The other flight attendants had just finished handing out snacks to their section. When they saw the blonde tossing me peanuts, they joined in the fun and started flipping their leftover peanuts into my lap as well.

I felt like a monkey at the zoo and I could have been offended, except I was really hungry. Hey, when there are three gorgeous beauties showering you with gifts, you just go with it. I mean, who could possibly have a problem with that?

Well, I will tell you who. As I sat there with 16 bags of peanuts in my lap, I turned to my wife and was met with an icy glare. "Did you flirt with her?" she inquired bluntly. I instinctively tossed her a couple bags of peanuts as a peace offering, ridiculously thinking this might appease her and answered an emphatic, "No". "You winked at her, didn't you?" she continued. I started to explain the pretzel situation, but that was met with a look that every husband dreads. The look that says: "I'm not buying what you're selling. It would be best for everyone if you shut up right now." So, I shut up and ate my peanuts. The peanuts were supposed to be free, but I sure was paying a high price for them.

For some reason, it seemed much colder on the plane the rest of the flight. (Time to close those air vents.) In fact, when we deplaned in Fort Myers, it was the chilliest 92 degrees I have ever experienced. Does my wife really believe I have the charisma and charm to just wink at a hot woman and she eagerly gives up all her goodies to me? Apparently so, but I assure you this is not how it usually works.

I know people will find this story hard to believe, so as evidence I present the one bag of peanuts remaining after I consumed the other bags on the vacation. The only other evidence I could present would be photos of those luscious stewardesses, er, I mean flight attendants. Of course, that would be the last photo I would ever take in my life. It would also be the last photo ever stored on my

iPhone, the iPhone 6. So I decided against taking any photos.

But this whole incident is just a major misunderstanding. There was no wink! No winking, no flirting, no nothing! It is so unfair that even when I try to do well, even when I exhibit exemplary behavior, that circumstances and my reputation ruin these efforts. This happens all the time! And trust me, I'm always innocent.

For the record: I swear I did not wink at that woman. I did not engage in a winking relationship with her. I was not making googly eyes at her. You believe me, don't you Jennifer? And Jan, you're with me on this, right? Jan? Jan?

Never Mess With A Woman's Closet

I was supposed to be working, but this click-bait was way too enticing to resist: This week on "Keeping Up With The Kardashians", Kayne West cleans out Kim's closet.

This show could be the most dangerous thing ever to appear on television. It is not in any way reality television; it is alternative reality television. I'm sure this episode is indeed faked and staged, but many men could die after viewing it. They need to run a disclaimer throughout the show: Do not try this at home. Disturbing a woman's closet could lead to severe injury or death. Because a husband should never, ever mess with a woman's closet. It is safer to poke a woman's most sensitive private part without permission than to penetrate her closet. At least if she gets enraged at the poke, you can claim you just wanted to spice up your love life, or even blame it on hormones. However, there is absolutely no excuse for touching the contents of her closet.

You should not look in it, you should not talk about it, you should pretend that you don't even know it exists. It is sacred territory, similar to an Indian burial ground. It is like the Ark of the Covenant – if you touch it, you will surely die. Indiana Jones would never enter a woman's closet, and Jack Bauer would definitely be afraid to go in there. "Tony, don't go in! The level of estrogen is too high. It will kill you instantly."

If you did trespass in your wife's closet and she killed you, she would serve no jail time. As long as there is one woman on the jury, she will not be convicted: "Yes, she did shoot him five times point blank in the head, cut his body into little pieces and then fed him to wolverines – but he entered her closet, so he had it coming to him. Not guilty, your honor."

I know this makes for good television because Kim's closet is larger than many apartments in Japan, which means Japanese viewers will be totally confused by this episode. Kim's closet must be wider than normal to accommodate Kim's clothes and the humongous booty that will be barely covered by these clothes. You need a wide door, a wide aisle, a super-wide mirror and enough space for Kim to spin around without causing structural damage to the entire house. It probably took a team of architects several weeks to design this closet.

I cannot believe that a person with Kanye's intellect would be stupid enough to mess with a woman's closet. I mean he's a great rapper, so he has to be very smart, right? But you have to be an idiot, and a special type of idiot at that, to mess with a woman's closet.

So this episode has to be fake because I'm guessing Kanye lives. But putting this totally unrealistic event on television is the epitome of irresponsibility. I am worried that young guys watching this episode will march into the bedroom and start rummaging through their wives' closets because they saw Kanye do it, so they believe it's acceptable. Again, this is one of the worst things you can ever do to a woman. So, let me be clear: NEVER, EVER, TOUCH ANYTHING IN YOUR WIFE'S CLOSET. Unless you are married to a Kardashian, then grab anything you can, any time you want. Even if you are a transvestite – Hands Off!

Marriage Is All About Hot Sex And Sammiches

My friend Bob Myers (not the Bob who causes me all the problems) passed away recently. Bob was one of the wisest men I have ever known. As a tribute, here is my favorite story about my remarkable friend.

My bachelor dinner had ended, and the guests were leaving. Bob walked over and motioned for me to bend down (keep in mind, he's short) because apparently, he had something important to tell me.

He said, "If you don't think about getting divorced more than three times the first year, you are doing well."

I looked at him skeptically, my jaw dropping. He just nodded, flashed a wry smile, said "good luck", and then quickly departed.

I was completely and utterly dumbstruck. This was the most ridiculous advice anyone had ever given to me. Think about divorce? No, my first year of marriage was going to be a blissful experience filled with hot sex and sammiches.

Why would there ever be any conflict? We were young and in love and that's all that matters. There would be no need for any arguments at all. Well, we might have a minor disagreement or two, but those would be quickly resolved. Afterwards, we would engage in some more hot sex after which my wife would make me a sammich.

And divorce? Are you crazy? Other couples might, but we are so much in love. No, this was going to be a perfect year filled with hot sex and sammiches. Hot sex and sammiches! Hot sex and sammiches! Yep, that's what I'm looking forward to.

One of two parts of a happy marriage

I did wonder why Bob would say something that preposterous. He had recently completed his first year of marriage, so maybe he did have some credibility. But his wife Julie was such a sweet, quiet, gentle woman. I couldn't even imagine Bob having any arguments or issues in his marriage. Yet, I still thought I was headed for marriage nirvana consisting of hot sex and sammiches. But then again, Bob was one of the wisest men I knew and he was nine years older than me, so I kept his advice in mind.

Now, I will never write about the details of my first year of marriage. Keep in mind, if you lock two young, stubborn, strong-willed people in a cage for a year and force them to function together, a tiny bit of conflict can occur.

So, it was around the fourth month of wedded blissfulness that my wife did something that really fizzed me off. Of course, I have no idea what it was. Maybe I was hungry and she claimed she was too tired to make me a – well you get the idea. But whatever it was, it was totally unacceptable. "I can't believe she did that," I fumed. This behavior is just terrible, and if it continues, I want a divor . . . Oh my! Suddenly Bob's words echoed in my head. But this was only one time and it probably was just a fluke, so I still thought he was crazy.

Until it happened again during the seventh month. All right, the first time wasn't just a fluke. Maybe Bob is on to something after all. But still, it's only twice. If my wife wouldn't keep doing stupid stuff to fizz me off, this wouldn't even be an issue.

In month eleven, I was rather startled the third time it occurred. Oh my! (yet again!) Maybe Bob knew what he was talking about after all. I had exhausted my "three-thought limit" and had a whole six weeks to go! Could I make it?

Fortunately, I did make it to the one-year anniversary with a "three-count" which meant I was doing well, according to Bob! And that wise man Bob was correct, because my marriage is still going. (And Bob's marriage lasted until death did he part.)

I must state that my wife had a much more difficult time during the first year of marriage than I did (if you read this blog regularly, you know I am stating the obvious). I admit I can be difficult to live with. Heck, sometimes I don't like living with myself. For my wife to keep an exact count of how many times I fizzed her off that first year, she would have needed one of those clickers designed for counting golf strokes. I think I finished over par for the year.

I am sure glad Bob did not give my wife any advice before the wedding. Being such a wise man, he probably would have told her: "I know this guy. Run out that door and don't stop until you cross the state line."

Therefore, I believe Bob's rule is highly accurate. However, I'm thinking with the changes in society over the many years since he developed the rule that maybe we can add a fourth time due to inflation. So, the Myers-Ake newlywed rule is this: "If you don't think about getting divorced more than four times the first year of marriage, you are doing well." As it is written, so shall it be done.

Tim's Christmas Budget

The Skinny: Now that I work from home, I do miss the funny interaction with office coworkers. Tim is a great guy and I really enjoyed working with him. He is also younger and thus, somewhat naïve. I'm not making fun of him, just telling a story . . .

Gather round, children. Your Uncle Don has another heartwarming Christmas story for you this year. This particular story is about Tim, but not Tiny Tim. This Tim could be tinier, but he always eats too much at the Chinese buffet.

It was a cold Friday in December when Uncle Don's coworker Tim arrived at work and proclaimed it was going to be an awesome day. Uncle Don and Erin (the guy with the huge beard from a previous post), who also shared that office, listened intently as Tim explained.

You see, last Christmas Tim's newlywed wife went out and

bought way too much stuff at Christmastime. She done rung up so many expenses on their credit card that they were still paying it off in June!

But that was not going to happen this year because Tim and his wife had discussed what she was going to buy, where she was going to buy it, and how much she was going to spend. His woman was now on a tight, I said tight, Christmas budget. Tim was excited because his wife had taken the day off to go Christmas shopping and carry out this carefully developed plan. Tim beamed with manly pride, chest puffed out, as he explained how he had gotten his woman under control.

Now in the olden days children, we probably would have never heard anything about this again, but now we live in the digital age – in the era of too much information.

So, a little bit past 10 a.m., the productivity and the peacefulness of the work environment were shattered . . .

"Why did she buy that stuff at Macy's? She was supposed to go to Target! The stuff is way cheaper at Target!" exclaimed Tim. I looked over to see Tim clutching his smartphone in both hands, grabbing it so tightly his forearms bulged. His jaw was clenched, his wide eyes staring at the screen in disbelief. That's right children, Tim had decided to track his wife's purchases in real time on the Internet. Smart guy that Tim.

"She probably went to Macy's because that's where her mother likes to shop," Tim speculated.

"She's shopping with her mother?" asked Erin.

"Yes," said Tim. "She likes to go Christmas shopping with her mother."

Erin and I then exchanged raised eyebrows and worried

looks. We knew Tim had a problem. Them women was shopping in packs, and nothing good ever comes of that children.

The one woman will see something and inquire, "Do you think I should buy this?" The answer from the other woman will always be, "Of course you should buy it! Why not?!", no matter what it is, no matter what is costs, no matter how bad a purchasing choice it may be, and ignoring any and all credit limits.

Now a guy would look at the very same situation and realize that if you even have to ask the question, then the answer is, "No, we can't afford it." Of course, men also make poor decisions when roaming in packs. Many a call from the police station has started off with: "Honey, the guys thought it would be a good idea to stop at the "Jiggle Club" on the way back . . . "

About an hour later, Erin and I were once again startled by . . . "She really overspent at that store! What did she buy that would cost that much?! JUST WHAT?"

"Maybe she bought your gift there. You wouldn't want to question that, would you Tim? You would look like such a jerk," warned Erin.

"Well, you might be right, but she is spending too much," said Tim as he left to get some coffee.

Of course, as soon as he was gone, Erin and I broke out in raucous laughter over his predicament. Now I know this constitutes laughing behind your friend's back which isn't very nice at Christmastime. However, the alternative would have been to laugh in his face. And of course, all this laughing was Erin's fault since your Uncle Don is a rather serious chap who rarely laughs at anything.

But then sometime around 12:30 p.m., there was some very encouraging news . . .

"Hey they've finished shopping! They just stopped for lunch on the way home. And get this, she's under budget!" proclaimed Tim enthusiastically. "But they did spend a lot on lunch, though."

"Lunch counts against the budget?" asked Erin.
"It does if she puts it on the credit card," said Tim sternly.

But Tim's optimism was soon shattered by a startling revelation . . .

"Wait a minute! They're not at the Appleby's near her mom's house. They're at the one in Monroe," gasped Tim.

"Isn't that the one right by that new mega strip mall?" asked Erin.

Oh no! Silence and dread then filled the office, children. Them women folk were not retiring, they were recharging.

Fortunately, Tim didn't check on his credit statement while we all went out for lunch, so we were able to enjoy the meal in peace and tranquility. We returned to the office and started back to work vigorously as we always did on a Friday afternoon.

But that highly productive work environment was regrettably disrupted again . . .

It was exactly 1:52 p.m. (I honestly did check my watch), when poor Tim literally threw his head down on his desk and pounded his fists.

"She's over, she went over!" Tim cried out in anguish. "It's over . . . (gasp) . . . it's o-o-o-over."

Erin and I exchanged a look of despair. We were morose, children; morose I tell you. There is no laughter when a man is defeated so decisively by his woman. Only gloom and misery. Of course, there was no consoling either because guys just don't do that type of thing. This is one of those instances that is so shameful, so devastating, it should forever remain a strict secret. It should never be spoken of again and under no circumstances should it ever be published in a book. Only a most despicable cad would do something like that.

Tim may have thought this was over, but unfortunately Tim's wife didn't consider it to be finished. Heck, it was only 2:00 p.m., plenty of time for more shopping, and the temptation of that new, big mega mall was just too much to resist. She made at least two more significant purchases. Each time work was interrupted by loud, mournful, painful sighs.

And each time I looked over to see Tim glaring into that smartphone, shaking his head. The final time, I think I may have heard Tim's credit card let out a yelp from his back pocket. It was either that or the burrito he had for lunch.

You see children, Tim's attempt at restraining his wife's Christmas spending failed miserably. His Christmas budget lay dead under his Christmas tree. But Christmas is not about ol' stupid budgets, children. It's about spending enormous amounts of money on stuff nobody needs because all the commercials and advertisements tell us we have to do that. Remember that Christmas is all about overcoming obstacles to reach our full potential and test our limits, especially our credit limits. It is about love, children, our exorbitant love of shopping and spending money.

And you see children, it was Tim's wife who understood the true meaning of Christmas, and not that fool Tim. Maybe someday he will learn, children, maybe someday he will learn.

Not An Afternoon Delight

The Skinny: The name and subject matter on this one are changed to protect the innocent. Hot Carla is a fictional character that is a composite of that neighbor who tends to show off her body.

I was busy working in my home office one afternoon when I was interrupted by the doorbell. I scurried downstairs to find my neighbor, Hot Carla, standing outside appearing distraught.

"I'm sorry to bother you, but I need someone to talk to," she explained.

I hesitated, then I nodded. I had important work to finish and of course I was a bit uncomfortable being alone inside with Hot Carla. I mean this is Hot Carla, and well, you know. But I invited her in since it seemed like the neighborly, Christian thing to do.

She thanked me, and assured me the discussion would not take long. I glanced at the clock. If we talked for 30 minutes, I could still finish my work on time. More importantly, my wife wasn't due home for another hour or so, and obviously Hot Carla had to be long gone by then. As she moved past me, I noticed she was wearing perfume. I made a mental note to spray some deodorizer around after she left. There could be no evidence that she had been in the house.

I directed her over to the loveseat and motioned for her to sit down, and I swear, she had in fact already started to sit. I turned my back, walked over to the far end of the couch, and sat where there would be a full seven feet of space between us. But apparently Hot Carla does not like a distance between people when discussing personal issues because she had not rested on the love seat. She waited until I was on the couch, then she kicked off her shoes and sat down right next to me. And "sat" is not the optimal term because she pulled her feet up off the floor behind her. So I guess she curled up next to me on the couch. Hot Carla had made herself comfortable and was now ready to talk. Me, I was feeling a bit uncomfortable at that moment.

Now this is not what you think (If it were, I wouldn't be writing about it, would I? And you are all totally disgusting for even going there). Hot Carla's father was ill and she needed some fatherly advice. She would typically be able to get that advice from her father, but obviously not in this case. So, I was serving the role of "father-figure". When young, attractive women value your paternal wisdom more than other male-type functions that you are able to perform, you know you are traveling down the hill, not up it. This realization is both uplifting, yet disturbing, at the same time.

Like many beautiful women, Hot Carla is oblivious to how hot she really is and what effect this particular seating arrangement might have on me. Therefore, Carla's intentions are innocent; she just wants to be this close to people when discussing very personal matters.

Now I know the guys out there are wondering how Hot Carla is dressed since she is "curled" inches away from me on the couch. I can say that it is summer, it is hot, and Hot Carla was dressed for coolness and comfort. So in the way of clothing; there wasn't much. She looked so hot I think I noticed some wisps of smoke emanating from her body. Carla may have been dressed to stay cool, but suddenly it was sweltering where I was seated, and I was seated way too close for comfort.

Now you might accuse me at this time of having impure thoughts, but this is absolutely not true. My thoughts were in fact totally pure – in the undiluted sense of the word. Even so, I was able to overcome this daunting obstacle. It takes a skilled listener with amazing super powers of concentration to perform under these circumstances. You must keep your mind and all your bones totally under control.

But I listened intently and was able to offer Hot Carla some good, fatherly-type advice. However, I was concerned that if the advice was too wise, and her father did croak, these meetings might become more frequent. A couple of times she was close to breaking down in tears. This would cause issues since I would feel the need to hug her. While this would be a comforting hug for her, it might have a different effect on me. But regardless, if the situation warranted, I was prepared to hug her for as long as necessary. The talk was now taking longer than I anticipated, and I needed to get back to work soon.

Fortunately, the conversation starting winding down. It had been a success. I was able to help this damsel in distress by comforting her and providing the guidance she so desperately needed.

Just knight me Sir Akealot. We must have been discussing something vitally important at that moment because I didn't notice any noise in the garage. By the time I heard the door open, it was too late to jump off the couch and propel my body through the air and onto that loveseat. If I just had a few seconds warning, I swear that's what I would have done.

In some cruel twist of fate, for some still unknown reason, my wife had decided, without warning I might add, to come home half-an-hour early that day. She had never done this before. I mean who leaves work a half hour early for no good reason? Who I ask? And yet, there I am sitting on the couch with a shoeless, Hot Carla, in all her hotness, curled up next to me, as I greet my wife.

There is no facial expression appropriate for this moment. The setting screams that I am guilty of inappropriate behavior, but my face can't say that. Also, I can't look too innocent because that implies I am trying to hide guilt. Instead, I go with a blank, somewhat bored look. "Sure, there's a hot, young, woman on the couch next to me. But, yawn, who's interested in that?"

I resist the urge to jump off the couch because that would appear suspicious. Instead, I slowly rise and move as carefully as an infantryman through a minefield, putting as much space between Carla and I as reasonably possible. At this moment, one wrong move, one wrong look, one wrong word, could cause an explosion of epic proportions.

"Carla's father is ill," I blurt out in attempt to defuse the tension. Fortunately, Carla's face communicates her distress. This would have been a great time for her to unleash those tears. I know I wanted to cry right then. It is helpful that Carla doesn't realize how this state of affairs (whoops, really bad word choice!) really appears. She is sweet, but can be blunt, and I could imagine her telling my wife, "Don't worry honey, we weren't screwing, we were only talking." My wife offers her sympathy and engages in some polite small talk. Since I don't return to the couch, fortunately Carla realizes the conversation is over. I walk her to the door keeping as much distance between us as I can.

And there will be no comforting hug as we part. Naturally, it would have been a polite, platonic, neighborly-type hug. The kind of hug you would give your sister (if I had a sister), and I'm sure I wouldn't have felt a thing. As I return, it seems the room temperature has dropped to around 10 degrees, and the air conditioner is not malfunctioning. I don't say a word the rest of the evening – and surprise! – I live to write about it.

Once again, I'm trying to do the right thing. I'm striving to use my special powers and skills for noble purposes. I'm giving of myself to promote love, peace, and the betterment of humanity. For the record, I want to state again that I am totally, totally, innocent. Really, really, I am. I was just trying to do the right thing, and the wrong thing happened . . . again.

📖 📖 📖

CHAPTER 9

Mumbo Jumbo

If a subject can be funny, I can find the humor in it. These essays are on topics that did not fit nicely into the other eight chapters, but they do belong in this book because they will bring a smile to your face. Enjoy!

Bad Drivers Need More Than Whispers

First, there was "The Horse Whisperer" who calmed wild horses. Then there was "The Dog Whisperer" who transformed unruly mutts. Now, AKE TV introduces the fabulous new reality show, "The Car Whisperer", who turns dangerous drivers into model motorists! Welcome to Episode #1!

Announcer: Meet Melvin Snerkly. Mr. Snerkly is regarded as the top driving instructor in the U.S. He has taught thousands of students over his esteemed 30 years in the business. He has taken the written driving test in all 50 states without missing a single question. He is easily recognized by his classic pocket protector and bow tie.

Today's problem driver is Carl "Crash" Craminski. Carl currently holds the record for License Violation Points in three different states. However, he is not popular with the insurance companies. Flo from Progressive once tried to kick him in the 'nads. The Geico gecko has flipped him off, and Jake from State Farm refuses to take his calls.

As our subject drives around the city, Melvin "The Car Whisperer" sits in the back seat, leans forward, and gently whispers words of instruction and encouragement. The goal is to turn our reckless driver into a model citizen of the road.

Melvin (in a very gentle, hushed tone): Yes Carl, check to make sure it's clear, then slowly back out.

[sound of tires squealing]
YAHHHHHHHHHHHH!

Okay, you just missed that car coming behind you, but that's all right. Now pull out onto the street making sure you give enough space to the cars approachi . . .

GEEEEEEEEEEEEEEEZ [tires screeching, horn blasting]
You also might want to turn down your stereo. Just because you enjoy crappy music, doesn't mean everyone else does. It will help you concentrate on driving, and unless you are deaf, you surely must be able to hear your music at a reasonable volume.

Now you are going to be turning right up here, so you should be getting into the right lane and signaling the turn. Get over, get over, get . . .

BAAAAAAAAAAAAAAAAA! [horn honking] [man cursing]
Okie dokie, the turn signal was invented in the 1930s and has been standard equipment since the 1940s. It's very easy to oper-

ate; down for left, up for right. It can "signal" your intention to turn which helps your fellow drivers. See, you can do it.

Ah, now you can make a right turn on red. It's clear, you can go. Go ahead. Still clear, what are you waiting for? . . . Okay, now you can't go because the left turn arrow on the other side is on. If you turn now, cars will be coming right at you, so don't go NOOOOOOOOOOOOOOOW!

PSSSSSSSSSSSSSSSSSSSST! [more horns]

Now you have the left turn arrow. That arrow pointing to the left means you can go left! It does, no fooling! So go, don't just sit there and stare at it, go, go, [massive horn honkings] Now the arrow's off. Don't turn now! Don't turn nooooooooooow

YOOOOOOOOOOOOOOOOOOOOOOOOOOWZA! [more horns] [more cursing]

Oh, here we are approaching an eight-lane, four-way stop. This is one of the most challenging driving situations around, Carl. Just slowly pull up to the intersection and stop, and I will talk you through . . .

RAAAAAAAZMAAAAAAAAAAAA! [multiple horns]

You see, a rolling stop is not actually a stop, because you never actually stop, get it? The stop sign is there to tell you to stop, and all those people honking their horns expect you to actually stop. Carl, please don't brake when approaching a green light. That's just not needed, and it irritates other people. You will have plenty of time to stop if the light changes. That's what the yellow caution light is for. It's been around since 1920, so you should have had sufficient time to adapt to it.

Now please stop talking on the cell phone. You are weaving all over the road. Okay now you are going straight, straight down the middle, and over the yellow line. [horrendous horn honking]. Now Carl, you really shouldn't give the finger to other drivers when it was your behavior causing the problem. It makes you look like a jerky numbskull. Uh, you are not providing an assured clear distance. Why are you so close to the next car? Why? Back off. He can't go any faster than the cars in front of him, can he? You need to back off in case he suddenly brakes.

WAAAAAAAAAAAAAAAAAAAAAAAAA! [severe screeching of tires]

Now it's time to get on the expressway and master some highway driving. Increase your speed on the on-ramp, signal, and then find a nice gap to merge safely into traffic. Hey, there's a swell space open behind the Buick, no behind, not in front, behind,

BE-HINDDDDDDD!
GAAAAAAAAAAAAARRRRR!

Carl, you're in the far-left lane, the speed lane, or passing lane. When you are in this lane, you need to maintain a faster pace so as not to impede other drivers who want to go faster. Now you're five miles per hour under the speed limit. Speed up, speed up, push the accelerator. Push it, push it. [honking]

Look in the rear-view mirror. See the traffic backed up 10 cars deep behind you? They want to go ahead of you, but they can't because you are hogging the lane. Look, look behind you. The rear-view mirror was invented in 1906 and every car has one. Either speed up or get out of the speed lane . . .

Just look for an open space to the right, and use your turn signal to indicate you are changing lanes. Whatever you do, just don't jerk the wheel to the right and [honking]

OHHHHHHHHHHHHH MYYYYYYYYYYYYYYY!

Ah, now you do need to pick a lane and stay in it. This one's good. Okay this one. How about this one. You really shouldn't pass on the right. Pick a lane….. please pick a lane, any lane just pick onnnnnnnnnnne!

Carl, you're in that car's "blind spot". It's called the blind spot because the driver is unable to see you in his mirrors. You need to speed up or slow down before that other car decides to change lanes . . .

HIJIMAMAAAAAAAAAAAAAAA!

All right, you are back in the speed lane and this time you are keeping pace with the traffic. Good boy, Carl. Ah, but see that sign? Your exit is coming up in two miles and you need to start moving over to the right lane. Go; start moving now.

You do understand your taxes paid for that sign and workers

put it up so you would know to get over and have plenty of time to respond. The exit sign is there so you will not need to suddenly cut across multiple lanes traffic to exit. And look! They even put up a second sign again informing you the exit is coming up just in case you missed the first one. So get over, change lanes, change lanes now.

Well, it's too late now. You can't make it with that big semi in the right lane. You will just have to get off at the next ex . . .

HOLLLLLEEEEEEEEEEEEE CRAAAAAAAAP!

Melvin (in normal voice): Let's find a restroom, I need to change my shorts. Turn left up ahead.

(Back in whisper-mode) Now, make a square turn. Don't just sweep across the lane because a car can pull up and . . .

AYE Yi Yiiiiiiiiiiiiiiiiiiiiiiiiiiiiiiii!!!!!!!!!!!!

Carl, it's called a turn because you are actually supposed to turn the steering wheel hand-over-hand, hand-over-hand.

Just pull into the space and park the car. Uh, well you see someone has gone to the trouble of painting these lines on the parking lot. You are expected to park between the lines, between the lines, not just wherever you want.

[after a quick bathroom break and change of underwear]

All right, you are not going to be able to make a left turn out of the parking lot. You cannot go across six lanes of traffic in rush hour. You can't even do that on Frogger, ha ha. So just make a riiiiiight.

WHOAAAAAAAAAAAAA NELLLLLLLLLLY!

Melvin: (Screaming) GET OUT OF THE CAR, CARL! GET OUT OF THE #@%!ING CAR, NOW! GIVE ME YOUR #^& *%#@ £€ LICENSE, SO I CAN BURN IT! YOU ARE NEVER, EVER, DRIVING AGAIN! AAAARGH!

Announcer: This concludes the premier episode of "The Car Whisperer". Unfortunately, there will not be an Episode #2.

Get A Flu Shot This Year Or Get Screwed

The Skinny: I find life funny, even when it's names of obscure flu viruses. I track the names of the flu viruses in the vaccine every year and found something humorous about the 2015-2016 version.

It's autumn! Time for colorful leaves, football, and of course, getting your flu shot. Every year at this time, we are told we must get a flu shot. Health experts tell us, "We are competent, scientific, medical scientists, well educated, in science, so we know what we are talking about. You must get the flu shot or you will get sick, very sick. If you get the flu, substances will shoot out of your bodily orifices in colors you never imagined possible. So get a flu shot, and get it right now!"

They also claim the flu shot is extremely effective in preventing the flu because these so-called scientists have carefully selected the targeted viruses for this year's vaccine using the most intelligent, supreme computer models available. They will not reveal the details of this process without having to kill you, but if you really want to see them, they've been posted online by Russian hackers.

So, last year I dutifully heeded this warning and drove 15 miles (to my wife's workplace), filled out paperwork, stood in line, and had a needle poked in my arm by a nurse who wasn't even "hot". And then in February, I ended up getting a bad case of the flu.

It seems last year's flu vaccine was not effective at all because it had targeted the wrong viruses. The Center for Disease Control (CDC) was forced to admit its "sophisticated computer model" was really a guy named "Phil" who sits over there in the corner, and that he had in fact "guessed wrong". After Phil quickly selected the viruses, he resumed playing Solitaire and watching Internet porn on his work computer.

Because everyone was puking their guts outs and destroying their undergarments, the CDC felt obligated to issue a statement that essentially said:

"Our bad, we might have guessed wrong or maybe the virus just mutated. We're not really sure. Remember, we did warn you that you would get real sick if you were infected by the flu virus, and we were right about that. So we do know what we are talking about since we are trained medical scientists and all that. If you have the flu, the best advice we have is to please try to refrain from dying. If too many people die, it will make us look bad, oh so bad, and stupid. This could cause our funding to be cut which would lead to even more deaths. So, please don't die. And remember, we use science, lots of science."

After last year's debacle, I was very interested in the flu viruses Phil chose for this year's vaccine. The first one is called, "A California". A California-type virus doesn't sound scary at all. It's probably a laid-back, hippie-type virus which lacks focus and commitment. It would rather be hanging out at the beach catching waves and smoking dope than causing disruptions in your body. When confronted by your immune system, it would say "Dude, okay, don't be so harsh, I'm leaving now. Stop attacking me, bro."

The second virus in the vaccine is the A Switzerland. This would seem like a gentle, peaceful virus which might cause a very mild case of the flu. A peaceful Swiss flu is unlikely to start a war in your intestines. And when confronted by your antibodies, this virus would quickly sign a peace treaty and leave you alone.

However, the third virus targeted by this year's vaccine is cause for extreme concern. It is the dreaded B Phuket virus (This is its real name, no fooling!). I fear if you contract the B Phuket virus, you will literally B Phuked. B Phuking alarmed! This is a virus with an attitude, a bad-@$$ attitude, and it doesn't care how sick it makes you.

The B Phuket is going to hit your body like a raging madman. Oh, you are going to get ill, extremely ill. You are going to feel Phuking awful. You are going to want it to Phuking stop. This virus is going to travel throughout your body shouting Phuket, Phuket, Phuket all! You will run a dangerously high fever because this virus will make you Phuking hot.

And a virus with an extreme, bad-@$$ attitude will literally give you a bad @$$. It will produce a nasty case of the Phuking sheetz. Your colon will soon catch fire and explode like fireworks on the Fourth of July. It will be a Phuking awesome display as flames and smoke pour out of your backside. The air will be thick and the odor Phuking intense. Your neighbors will call the EPA about an unknown toxic substance in the air. Your can of Glade will be cowering in the back corner of your closet. Your intestines will "B" all Phuked up, yes they will.

Your immune system is no match for a virus this repulsive. When your antibodies show up to confront it, it will shout "Phuk you! I'm the Phuking B Phuket virus and I'm telling you to Phuk off right now. Phuket, Phuket, B Phuket!" This will scare the pi$$ right out of your protective blood cells which will escape on the next yellow river ride out of town.

That's why I am so alarmed about the B Phuket virus. Let me tell you, I want that Phuking flu vaccine and I want it Phuking now! I am not a medical professional, but I am recommending everyone get the flu shot this year, so you don't get B Phuket. And be sure to remember to tell the nurse you came there to B Phuked. I'm sure she will then be extra gentle with the needle.

I've warned you – consider this a public service announcement.

The Fat: Fortunately, this flu virus was much more effective than the previous version and no one caught the B Phuket flu.

I Don't Give Up My Blood Easily

"Don?"

My head snapped up and I nodded as I made my way across the

waiting room. It was time for my annual blood test to check my cholesterol levels.

But there was something wrong, very wrong. This phlebotomist (blood drawer) was unlike any I had seen before. He was in fact, a guy. I strongly prefer a female phleby (my term, never call them that to their face). If this sounds sexist and old-fashioned, it's only because it is sexist and old-fashioned.

But I have my reasons. I consider this a semi-intimate experience. It is not an actual exchange of bodily fluids, but the phleby is taking fluids from me while in close physical contact. At my age, I'll take all the action I can get.

Also, it's very important that I am distracted from the act of a sharp needle being jabbed into my arm and precious blood being sucked out of my body. (More on this in a moment.) So, my ideal phleby is a young, friendly woman who engages me in pleasant conversation to totally distract me from the dastardly thing she is doing to my arm.

I don't want her to be too attractive because I don't want to be tempted to flirt, lest I say something offensive just before she sticks me with the needle. If I happen to fizz her off, that needle could get jabbed much harder and deeper than necessary.

But the last thing I want is a smoking-hot phleby, playfully tying that strap around my arm and whispering reassuring comments in my ear. Yes, I do want to be distracted, but not too much:

"Oh Mr. Ake, there is not any blood in your arm!
Where did it all go?
Me: (Embarrassed look on my face, glancing downward.)

"Oh my, Mr. Ake! Now how are we going to get all
that blood out of there and back into your arm?
Me: "Uh, I do have a couple of ideas."

Then she takes the needle, thrusts it into my leg, full force – and twists it.

You are probably wondering why I am so particular about having my blood drawn. What's the big deal? Okay, I must admit I get a little squeamish during the procedure. Alright, let me restate that. I get SQUEAMISH, extremely SQUEAMISH. I realize this is not manly behavior, but it's involuntary and highly frustrating.

This has happened since I was young and has only improved slightly with age. If I think about that needle sticking in my arm, I become ill. I do not pass out; I break out in a profuse sweat which starts at my head and ends up drenching my entire body. I feel woozy for the rest of the day, and it takes at least 24 hours to totally rehydrate. That is why it's extremely important that I am fully distracted during the procedure. If I don't think about what is happening, I am able to get though it fine.

Unfortunately, the vein in my arm is not very pronounced. This is not a problem for a skilled phleby, but a major problem for an inept one. If there is a problem during the blood draw, I start thinking about the needle and a sweaty meltdown ensues. So, I need a phleby who can distract me and get the blood out smoothly on the first try.

Not only wasn't this phleby a woman, but there were other issues. I gave him the nickname "Pokey" (not actually spoken) based on his appearance and demeanor. Pokey was chubby, frumpy, his clothes somewhat disheveled and his hair was tousled. Not the image you want to project as a medical professional. He did wear a lab coat, but it was at least a size too small. Fantastic! Chris Farley is about to draw my blood. This was going to be Awwwwesome.

I had no confidence in Pokey at all. I was extremely anxious, and I hadn't even seen the needle yet. My instincts told me to run away screaming like a little girl, but that would have been embarrassing. So, I told myself everything was going to be fine. Pokey had received training, right? He could do the job! But the nickname "Pokey" turned out to be pretty accurate.

I sat down and extended my arm expecting impending doom. I had to conduct an important webinar in three hours and suddenly realized that maybe I should not have scheduled my blood draw for today. Duh!

Pokey began the procedure. However, there was no pleasant conversation to distract me. Pokey wasn't skilled at social interaction since he probably had spent a great deal of his life playing video games. But this was not Pokémon, it was pokey me.

He failed to draw any blood on his first attempt. Unfortunately, it was too late to bolt, although I so much wanted to run. I thought he got it on try two, but then I heard him mumble. Mumbles are never good; positive things are never mumbled, only bad things.

"Is there something wrong?" I asked.

"The vein rolled and I can't get the blood out," he whined. What I wanted to say is: "No, the vein did not roll. You are just an incompetent slob." But I didn't say a word because he still had to poke me again.

"Try the vein in my hand," I suggest. (I know to do this from experience.)

"The hand?"

I nod (while I think: yes, you moron, the hand).

He grabs my hand eagerly and then squeals, "You have a nice vein in your hand!" (Count Dracula shows the same enthusiasm with necks.)

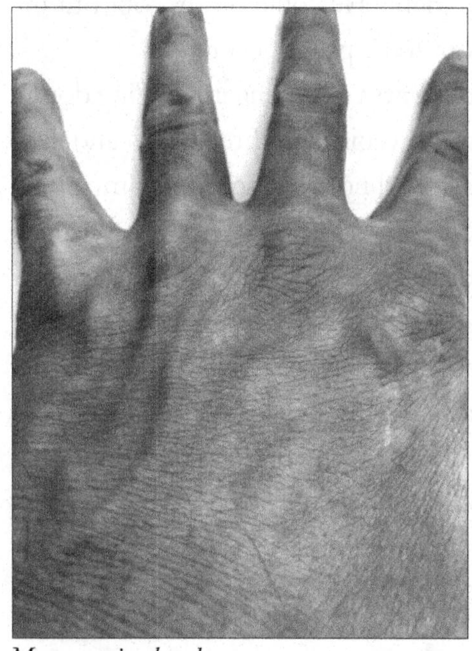

My very veiny hand

I think: Whoa Pokey! Easy with the hand. Settle down boy, you are just drawing my blood. We are not going steady.

He sticks the needle in my hand and exclaims, "The blood is coming out!"

Unfortunately, this sequence of events has caused me to think about the needle, and my shaved head begins to get hot and clammy. Here comes the sweat; the meltdown has started. I begin internally screaming, telling myself that the danger has passed and that ol' nasty needle is no longer in my body. There is no reason to get sick now.

Fortunately, this self-talk works. I stabilize and have only a "partial meltdown". My head is covered with sweat, but that's all. However, I am still somewhat ill, and I slump forward, holding my head in my hands.

"Are you okay?" Pokey asks.

(Do I look okay, moron?)

"I will be alright. I just need some water," I reply.

And do I need water, and now. When I am having a "meltdown", water provides me with tremendous physical and psychological benefits. Water prevents the sweating from spreading, and instantly makes me feel 1000% better.

"I will try to find some water," Pokey says.

What! You will try to find some water? Where the heck are we – some freakin' Third World country?

"I am verli, verli, sorree. Der has been no rain and all da wells are dry . . . "

Or maybe in the Old West – "Thar's been an awful drought, but Clem's fixing to git out his divining rod and find you a spring!" Instead of immediately getting the water, Pokey asks me something else which I can't even remember. I reply that I need water, now! He repeats that "he will try to find some" and then finally goes on his search.

As I wait, I wonder – since he is a millennial, does he think water only comes from plastic bottles and that is why he needs to search for it? Maybe I should have instructed him that they call it "tap water" because it comes from a tap.

Pokey finally returns from his quest with a paper cup. The cup is not full, and the water is not cold, but it does the job. I leave with a heavy bandage on my arm and another on my hand. It looks like I lost a fight, and, in a way, I did.

I made it through the webinar, and you'll be happy to know my cholesterol levels are exemplary! I can't wait to do this again next year!

The Fat: Ironically, the next year my doctor used a new test which provides a complete cholesterol profile with only a finger stick. For me, this is one of the greatest technological breakthroughs ever!

The Prayer That Almost Ruined Christmas

Gather round children (all you adult children, that is), your Uncle Don has another heartwarming Christmas story that is sure to become a holiday classic. Christmastime is all about miracles, children, and this here miracle happened just last year.

I was pleased to see in my email the invitation to my writing club's annual Christmas party. I had attended last year and had a most splendid time. There was a delicious potluck dinner and much festive fellowship of the season.

And we call it a Christmas party, children. None of that political correct crap for us; because it's not a holiday party, it's a Christmas party. This saying "Happy Holidays" instead of "Merry Christmas" is just plain silly. Flag Day is a holiday. So, when I say Happy Holidays, I am wishing you a joyous Flag Day in December when Flag Day is actually in June. Now tell me that isn't just plain stupidity, children, just plain stupidity.

But I feared calling it a Christmas Party this year could present a problem. Hannah was a relatively new member, and one of my best friends in the club. She is a fine writer and a wonderfully pleasant woman. But Hannah had a secret, children, a secret that few members of the group knew about.

I had read some peculiar posts on Hannah's Facebook page. There was something different about her. I confronted her about my suspicions in private after last month's meeting.

"Are you Jewish?" I asked.

"Yes, I am." answered Hannah.

Now, I think it's wonderful to have Hannah in the club. One of the best things about this group is you meet a wide variety of different people who are all united by their love of writing. I only asked her this question because she is my good friend, and friends share that type of stuff.

But now we had invited a Jewess to a "Christmas" Party. I hoped so much that she would attend, but I worried she might stay home. I thought about emailing her, but what would I say? "Hey, I know it says "Christmas" Party, but Jews are welcome, too!" Awkward, very awkward, children.

Now, I have a strategy for potluck dinners, children. I buy a bag of off-brand chips at the dollar store. Yes, they may be greasy and stale, but I don't care because I'm not eating that crap. Then I arrive early so I can sneak my cheap chips on the table without being seen by too many people. Finally, at dinnertime, I stuff my face with all the expensive shrimp and fancy cheeses other people bring. When you do the math: $10 worth of classy food minus $1 of stale chips equals "Free Appetizers". Score!

I was delighted to see Hannah walk through the door. I rushed over to greet her.

Me: I will wish you a Happy Hanukkah, if you wish me a Merry Christmas.
Hannah: Merry Christmas!
Me: Happy Hanukkah!

Then we embraced in a cross-religious, unification, diversity-type hug. That's how it should always be, children. We should be able to celebrate our differences and not hide behind all that "Happy Holidays" junk.

The party was going wonderful, children, until Stella announced it was time to eat. Then she said the horrific words that threatened to ruin the entire night, and even Christmas itself:

"Everyone bow their heads, Hannah is going to say the blessing for our meal."

WHAT? Back up the sleigh, Santa! Hannah is giving the Christmas prayer?

My head came close to exploding: A JEW IS SAYING THE PRAYER FOR OUR CHRISTMAS DINNER!

I strive to be as tolerant and inclusive as I can, children, but I do have my limits, and this was just way too much. There are no circumstances or conditions that exist where it would be permissible for a Jew to give the Christmas blessing. This was wrong, so very wrong.

I thought about speaking up, shouting "Stop the prayer. Abort, abort, she is a Jew!" But Hannah had already begun to pray, and it would be highly inappropriate and rude to interrupt at this point. Besides, I was famished, and somebody needed to eat all those delicious shrimps.

I thought about the negative consequences of this prayer. There was no way that God was going to ever bless a Christmas meal prayed over by a Jew. He would more likely curse it. Well, in that case, I'm sure as heck not eating the egg salad. I can see the headline in tomorrow's paper: Ten Hospitalized With Salmonella Due To Jewish Prayer At Christmas Dinner.

I was distressed by the situation. It was unacceptable. It was un-American. There is no place in the Christmas story for any Jews and, therefore, a Jew should not be praying at a Christmas celebration.

To make things even worse, I noticed someone had brought ham to the dinner. A nice Black Forest variety, thinly sliced, great sammich-making meat. I'm fairly certain that a Jew should not be blessing ham. A single prayer that violates tenets of two major religions at the same time cannot be a good thing.

Fortunately, I wasn't going to be cursed by this prayer because I wasn't praying. Stella's announcement was so shocking that I didn't even bow my head. No, sir. Instead, I stared intently at Hannah, carefully dissecting and evaluating every word she prayed.

I had never heard a Jew pray before, so I did not know what

to expect. However, my former years in the Baptist church made me more than qualified in identifying a good meal-blessing prayer. But, by now Hannah was halfway into the prayer, and there was something peculiar about it. It started off like a normal Christian prayer and so far, it sounded good, it sounded right. I was certain though at any moment she would mention a menorah and throw in some strange sounding Yiddish terms, all starting with the letter "Y".

As she continued, unbelievably, it still was indistinguishable from a good Baptist meal blessing. But we were nearing the end of the prayer when she would have to state exactly who we were praying to. Hannah was fast approaching a literal "come to Jesus" moment because you can't have a Christmas prayer without mentioning the baby Jesus – just ask Ricky Bobby.

My throat tightened, and I held my breath as the prayer came to the end. We had reached the moment of truth.

Then a miracle happened, children. An actual, wonderful Christmas miracle, right there in that room.

In concluding the prayer, Hannah went "full Jesus" on us. Not just "baby in the manger Jesus", oh no, she went "savior of the world Jesus", and even ended the prayer in Jesus' name.

It was a mericle, children. It was a wonderous Christmas mericle! But how, how, was it even possible? How could a Jew pray like that? Except for the fact it was delivered by a woman, strict, old-school, Baptist Deacons would have given this prayer very high marks.

I was so stunned that I stared across the room at Hannah in utter disbelief. She saw my expression. Being irritated at my reaction, she mouthed "What?" back at me. I wanted to yell across the room, "Nice prayer, Jew girl!" but thought better of it. I was so dumbfounded that I even forgot to get to the front of the line, which meant that scoundrel Dave got to the shrimp before I did. I bet that cheapskate is the one who brought the hard, stale, day-old muffins for dessert. I did manage to get a couple shrimp as well as exotic cheeses and some of that ham. I even ate some egg salad, but only a couple bites because, well, I still had my concerns.

After dinner, I confronted Hannah and asked her how a Jew could pray like that. She told me she happened to be a Messianic Jew. Well, I certainly agree. You have to be one messed up Jew to participate in antics like that.

But the beautiful thing, children, is that Christmas was saved. Christmas could have been ruined by this prayer, but God intervened by a miracle to send his Son as a baby into this prayer and save it. I can't remember where, children, but I think I've heard a story similar to this one somewhere before.

To all my readers and friends: Peace on Earth, Goodwill to All Men!

📖 📖 📖

Acknowledgments

This book is not possible without the faithful readers of Ake's Pains blogs. My "people" are the best and provide encouragement to produce quality material even when I am tired, rushed and cranky. More thanks to my editor, Sandie Hampton, who polished the rough blog posts into a shiny finished product.

My Art Director, Michael Gorfido, created another outstanding, attractive, eye catching cover using the dynamic photography of Craig James. I am blessed to have such talented friends and associates. I also need to thank the members of The Write Stuff authors group and The Writers Group (Akron) for their support. A special thank you to author H.L. Gibson for providing the subtitle: "Musings from a brilliant idiot". She was attempting to describe my writings and said, "You're an idiot, but you're a brilliant idiot." I can't say it any better than that.